soup

Anne-Catherine Bley

# soup

photographs by Akiko Ida

whitecap

Soupe poche

Velouté glace a

Bloody Mary

Soupe Froide

Soupe du

It all started several years ago, when I was living in Paris. I had dreams of finding a place that served light, healthy, great-tasting food—the type packed with vegetables, and that, above all, was a far cry from "diet food." But I more or less drew a blank. Then, one day, I struck lucky! I discovered the New York soup bar in an episode of the television series, "Seinfeld." Some time later, I visited New York myself and saw, and even tasted, some of those soups. They were exactly what I'd like to find in Paris! So, because there was nothing like it in France, I decided to venture into the catering business—a major first for me—and set up my own Soup Bar.

While preparing for the restaurant opening, I set about perfecting "my" recipe book. I honestly didn't expect to come across so many recipes or such originality. For nearly a year, I made two or three different soups a week and tried them out on my friends and family. After this trial period, I hadn't been disinherited and my friends weren't making excuses to avoid coming to dinner, which was encouraging! I "altered," adapted, and modified the recipes, adding this and taking out that... so they eventually became MY recipes. Now, they're yours. You can follow every step scrupulously, make changes, or substitute an ingredient you don't have for one that's been lurking at the back of your refrigerator. Don't be intimidated! Soups are easy to make, they're good for you and, above all, they're anything but boring!

Anne-Catherine Bley

# buying and using vegetables

## fresh vegetables

Buy them at the market, from the greengrocers or at the supermarket. It's a good idea to check the labels for their place of origin, as this will give you a better idea of their quality. If a vegetable has come a long way before landing on the shelves, it's a pretty good bet that it was picked while it was still ripening so that it wouldn't spoil during transportation. I'd recommend buying your vegetables at the market, preferably from a local producer—look out for the sign on their stalls. Their products are grown locally (so they don't have to travel) and are ultra-fresh. On occasion, market gardeners can also offer you unusual varieties. The vegetables you buy from other outlets will have passed through the hands of a wholesaler (or central purchasing department). They've usually been kept in a cold room for some time. Some products can be kept fresher for longer in a cold room, as is the case, for example, with pumpkins: they're harvested in the fall and winter, but can be found in the stores as late as April. Their thick skin makes them very robust and they can be kept for several months. Some imported vegetables end up in refrigerated storage. This means they can be bought all year round—the height of convenience, without a doubt, but often at the expense of flavor!

## frozen vegetables

I'm saddened by the thought that some children must believe that spinach is a brick-shaped vegetable that only comes in hard green lumps in a plastic bag. However, I'm the first to eat frozen spinach or peas with relish all year round. There's nothing wrong with frozen vegetables: they are usually very high quality and, above all, very easy to use. No peeling, chopping, or slicing—everything has already been done for you. No one's going to argue with that! The range of products is huge and doesn't depend on the season. There's only really one no-no for me: I don't recommend the use of frozen herbs, which really do lose most of their taste.

## canned vegetables

I use canned vegetables on occasion: when I need chickpeas, red kidney beans, button mushrooms, chestnuts, and corn. Also, when I need tomatoes, because I have a problem with the fresh variety—what you get, 99 percent of the time, is a perfectly round, perfectly smooth, perfectly tasteless vegetable. So, if I can't lay my hands on tomatoes grown in the open fields or the garden—tomatoes which have a few dents, which have even burst open, which are more red than yellow or green—then I prefer to use canned tomatoes, which have often been picked in southern climes and really taste like tomatoes should.

## some tricks of the trade

### Chestnuts

To prepare fresh chestnuts, score the shell and immerse them in boiling water for 5 minutes. After that, the hardest thing is to peel off the outer shell and inner skin while they're still hot! However, for the holiday seasons—even all year round in some supermarkets—vacuum packed or canned chestnuts, even frozen ones, are readily available.

### Spinach, sorrel, nettles, etc.

These green vegetables in particular must be very thoroughly washed to remove any traces of soil. A fairly large high-sided cooking pot should be used to cook them because they start out in such a big volume. After cooking for 5 minutes, only a small amount of greens will be left at the bottom of the pan.

### Dried vegetables

The recipes in this book are made with red, yellow, and green lentils, which are now widely available. When the recipe calls for green lentils, don't stint yourself—use Puy lentils from France. When I need chickpeas and kidney beans, I save a little cooking time by using the canned variety, which are pre-cooked. Don't forget to rinse them first in clean water.

### Leeks

Leeks also have to be thoroughly washed, as dirt gets lodged even in the innermost parts. The best way to do this is to make four cuts lengthways from the green top down almost to the root, so that the leek looks like a feather duster. Hold it under running water, fanning it out to clear out all the sand and soil.

### Pumpkin, okra

There are quite a few varieties of pumpkin with different names and different shapes—winter squash, squash—although they all taste very similar. Okra is a close cousin to the pumpkin, with slightly chestnutty flesh. Pumpkin skin (if using) should be well scrubbed—it's also very thick so you'll need a sharp knife.

### Potatoes

To achieve a smooth, even purée in soups where potatoes are an ingredient, always use potato varieties known as "boiling potatoes" that will mash well, such as Yukon Gold for instance.

# cooking, storage

## kitchen tools

### For cooking

All you need is a large saucepan and a deep pan or stockpot, or a pressure-cooker large enough to hold the finished soup, and a well-fitting lid. Using a pressure-cooker reduces the cooking time. You don't need to use non-stick equipment as soups are made with a large quantity of water.

### For blending

• Food mill: this hand-driven appliance involves using a few more utensils because you'll have to decant the puréed soup into another receptacle. The different plates supplied allow you to make a fairly smooth, fine soup, but are not very satisfactory for preparing very coarse soups like borscht or gazpacho.
• Electric blender: this is perfect for making cream soups and very fine, smooth soups. However, like the food mill, it's not suitable for making coarser soups with an even consistency.
• Hand-held or immersion blender (sometimes called a "stick blender"): this is my favorite tool. Not only is it very practical because it can be used directly in the saucepan, but it also can be washed and stored very easily—and it allows you to obtain the desired consistency without over-blending.

## storage and freezing

There's no problem keeping fresh soup in the refrigerator for a few days—usually from 3-5 days, depending on the ingredients. Some vegetables, like cabbages, potatoes, and peas, are more delicate and can "turn." Soup that has gone off has a slightly sour taste and should be tossed straight into the garbage.
You need to observe a few simple rules when freezing soup:
- Divide the soup into several small containers (1-2 people), so that you don't need to defrost more than necessary;
- Uncooked soups (such as gazpacho) are not suitable for freezing. They contain chunks of vegetables (cucumber, peppers) which are full of water molecules. As a result, they lose their crunchiness when defrosted and the soup looks very unappetizing!
- Cream soups, which are thoroughly blended to a purée, are the best soups to freeze.

tomato soups

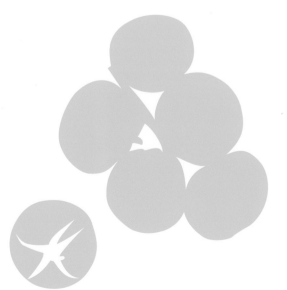

# tomato soups

## cream of tomato soup

PREPARATION TIME: 10 MINUTES / COOKING TIME: 25 MINUTES

1 Tbsp (15 mL) olive oil
1 onion, peeled and finely sliced
2 cloves garlic, peeled and finely chopped
2 Tbsp (30 mL) tomato paste
2 lb (1 kg) very ripe tomatoes, peeled (see Tip below),
   and chopped (or 1 x 28-oz/796-mL) can tomatoes)
1 bay leaf
1 sprig thyme
sugar
1 cup (250 mL) water
½ cup less 1 Tbsp (100 mL) whipping cream
salt

Heat the olive oil in a deep pan and lightly brown the onion. Add the garlic and tomato paste, followed by the tomatoes. Tie the bay leaf and thyme together (fastening the other end of the string to the pan handle is the best way to avoid leaving this bouquet garni in the soup before blending). Add a pinch of sugar and season with salt. Pour in the measured water and bring to a boil. Turn down the heat, cover with a lid, and leave to simmer for 15-20 minutes. Remove the bouquet garni and blend the soup to a smooth purée. Stir in the cream and adjust the seasoning, to taste.

TIP
To peel fresh tomatoes: make a small slit at the stalk end, bring a saucepan of water to a boil, remove from the heat, and plunge the tomatoes into the boiling water for 30 seconds. Drain and refresh in cold water. The skins should peel off easily.

## variations on cream of tomato soup

You can spice up cream of tomato soup in a variety of different ways. The basic principle is simple: make the Cream of Tomato Soup with the recipe on page 12, then "garnish" it with spices, fresh herbs, or other ingredients. Below are four serving suggestions, but you can give free rein to your imagination and come up with your own variations.

### cream of tomato soup with cilantro

**+ 1 small bunch fresh cilantro, rinsed, leaves stripped and coarsely chopped**

Just before serving the soup, stir 3/4 of the chopped cilantro into the soup and scatter the rest over the top as a garnish.

### cream of tomato soup with bacon

**+ 5 oz (150 g) bacon, finely diced**
**+ 1 Tbsp (15 mL) Marsala (or Madeira, sherry...)**

Lightly fry the bacon until nicely browned, then deglaze the skillet with the Marsala. Add the bacon to the soup just before serving.

### cream of tomato soup with ginger

**+ 2 thumb-sized pieces of fresh ginger, peeled and finely chopped**

Lightly brown the ginger with the onion at the start of the recipe.

### cream of tomato soup with mozzarella

**+ 1 big ball of mozzarella cheese, sliced**
**+ several basil leaves, rinsed and finely chopped**

Just before serving the soup, cut each mozzarella slice into four or six pieces. Add them to the soup and sprinkle with the chopped basil.

## cream of tomato soup with meatballs

PREPARATION TIME: 20 MINUTES / COOKING TIME: 30 MINUTES

¼ lb (125 g) ground beef
2 Tbsp (30 mL) cumin seeds
2 onions, (1 finely chopped, 1 thinly sliced)
1 egg yolk
2 Tbsp (30 mL) olive oil
2 cloves garlic, peeled and finely chopped
2 Tbsp (30 mL) tomato paste
2 lb (1 kg) very ripe tomatoes, peeled (see page 12),
   and chopped (or 1 x 28-oz/796-mL can tomatoes)
1 bay leaf
1 sprig thyme
sugar
1 cup (250 mL) water
½ cup less 1 Tbsp (100 mL) whipping cream
salt, freshly ground black pepper

Mix together the ground beef, cumin seeds, the finely chopped onion, and the egg yolk in a large bowl. Chill in the refrigerator for at least 15 minutes. Heat 1 Tbsp of olive oil in a deep pan and lightly brown the thinly sliced onion. Add the garlic and tomato paste, fry for a minute or two, then stir in the tomatoes.

Tie the bay leaf and thyme together with string and add to the pan (fastening the other end of the string to the pan's handle is the best way to avoid leaving this bouquet garni in the soup when blending). Add a pinch of sugar and season with salt. Pour in the measured water and bring to a boil, then turn down the heat, cover with a lid, and allow to simmer for 15-20 minutes. Remove the bouquet garni. Blend the soup to a smooth purée. Stir in the cream and adjust the seasoning, to taste.

While the soup is cooking, roll the ground beef mixture into small balls in your palm. Heat the remaining olive oil in a skillet and fry the meatballs until cooked through. Season with salt and pepper. Add the meatballs to the tomato soup and reheat for approximately 5 minutes to allow their flavors to mingle well with the tomatoes.

# tomato soups

## tomato and red bell pepper soup

PREPARATION TIME: 15 MINUTES / COOKING TIME: 30 MINUTES

1-2 Tbsp (15-30 mL) olive oil
1 large onion or 2 medium onions, peeled and finely sliced
4 cloves garlic, peeled and chopped
2 red bell peppers, finely sliced into strips
1$^3$/4 lb (875 g) very ripe tomatoes, peeled (see page 12) and
   finely sliced (or 1 x 28-oz/796-mL can tomatoes)
2 Tbsp (30 mL) tomato paste
2 cups (500 mL) water
basil leaves
salt, freshly ground black pepper

Heat the oil in a deep pan and lightly brown the onion and garlic. Add the bell peppers and cook until soft. Add the tomatoes, tomato paste, and measured water. Season with salt and allow to simmer over low heat until the soup thickens (about 25 minutes). Remove from the heat, add basil leaves to taste, and blend the soup to a very smooth purée. Adjust the seasoning to taste.

pumpkin soups

# pumpkin soups

## cream of pumpkin soup

PREPARATION TIME: 10 MINUTES / COOKING TIME: 30 MINUTES

2 tsp (10 mL) olive oil
2 onions, peeled and thinly sliced
1 clove garlic, peeled and thinly sliced
2$\frac{1}{2}$ lb (1.2 kg) pumpkin (or 1$\frac{3}{4}$ lb/875 g pumpkin flesh), peeled,
   seeded, and cut into chunks
3 cups (750 mL) water
$\frac{1}{2}$ cup less 1 Tbsp (100 mL) whipping cream
nutmeg
salt

Heat the oil in a deep pan, and lightly fry the onions and garlic for about 5 minutes, until the onions are transparent. Add the pumpkin flesh, followed by the measured water and some salt. (The pumpkin contains water, so there's no need to cover it completely with the cooking water, but you should give it a stir once or twice while cooking). Bring to a boil, then turn down the heat and cook until the pumpkin flesh is soft (about 25 minutes).

Before puréeing the vegetables, set aside some of the cooking water, in case you need to thin the soup. Blend into a very smooth purée, adding all or part of the reserved cooking water to obtain the desired consistency. Stir in the cream, add a little freshly grated nutmeg, and adjust the seasoning to taste.

# pumpkin soups

## variations on cream of pumpkin soup

Cream of pumpkin soup makes an ideal base for all kinds of different combinations—this mild, creamy vegetable goes well with all kinds of flavors, whether on the sweet side or highly spiced. Why not have a bit of fun and experiment?

### cream of pumpkin and cinnamon soup

**+ 2 tsp (10 mL) ground cinnamon**

Sprinkle the cinnamon over the onions and garlic when browning them in the olive oil.

### cream of pumpkin and chestnut soup

**+ 1 lb (500 g) fresh chestnuts or 1 can of chestnuts in water**

Score the shells of the chestnuts then scald them for 5 minutes. Drain, and peel the shells and skin. Cook in a little salted water in a covered saucepan for 10-15 minutes. Coarsely chop a few of the chestnuts and set aside for garnish. Add the cream, nutmeg, and any further seasoning to the puréed pumpkin, followed by the rest of the piping hot chestnuts. Blend all to a coarse purée. Garnish the soup with the reserved chopped chestnuts.

### cream of pumpkin and coconut soup

**+ 1 half-thumb-sized piece of fresh ginger, peeled and finely chopped
 or 1 tsp (5 mL) freshly grated ginger**
**+ 2 tsp (10 mL) ground cinnamon**
**+ 3/4-1 cup (175-250 mL) coconut milk**

Lightly brown the ginger with the onions, garlic, and cinnamon. After puréeing the pumpkin, add the coconut milk and all or part of the reserved cooking water to obtain the desired consistency. Purée again, then add the cream, grate in a little nutmeg and adjust the seasoning, as for the original recipe.

### cream of pumpkin soup with ravioli

**+ 1 package fresh ravioli**
**+ 2/3 cup (150 mL) grated Gruyère cheese**

Just before serving, bring a saucepan of salted water to a boil and add the ravioli. As soon as they are cooked and float to the surface, drain, and stir them into the pumpkin soup. Ladle the soup into bowls and sprinkle with grated Gruyère cheese.

# pumpkin soups

### cream of okra soup with bacon
PREPARATION TIME: 10 MINUTES / COOKING TIME: 30 MINUTES

2 lb (1 kg) okra (ladyfingers)
2 tsp (10 mL) olive oil
2 onions, peeled and sliced
4 cups (1 L) water
3½ fl oz (100 mL) whipping cream
nutmeg
5 oz (150 g) sliced bacon
salt

Clean the skin of the okra thoroughly, then seed and slice them into rounds without removing the skin. (You'll need a good knife with a strong blade because okra skin is very tough, although it becomes really soft when cooked). Heat the oil in a deep pan and lightly brown the onions for several minutes. Add the okra, measured water, and a little salt. Bring to a boil, then turn down the heat and leave to simmer until the flesh of the okra is soft. Blend the soup to a purée and stir in the cream. Grate in a little nutmeg and check the seasoning. Broil the bacon slices, brushed with a little oil, until crispy and use them as a garnish when serving.

TIP
At the height of the okra season, when they're very ripe, you won't need to add any cream as the flesh is creamy enough.

### cream of pumpkin soup with fresh mussels
PREPARATION TIME: 25 MINUTES / COOKING TIME: 35 MINUTES

2 quarts (2 L) fresh mussels, scrubbed and
  "beards" removed
3 cups (750 mL) water
2 tsp (10 mL) olive oil
4 shallots, peeled and sliced
2¾ lb (1.2 kg) pumpkin (or 1¾ lb/875 g pumpkin flesh),
  peeled, seeded and cut into chunks
½ cup less 1 Tbsp (100 mL) whipping cream
½ cup (125 mL) white wine (optional)
flat-leaf parsley, coarsely chopped
salt, freshly ground black pepper

Put the mussels in a pan with the measured water and cook on high heat until they have all opened. (It's important to discard any that have remained shut.) Drain the mussels and strain the cooking liquid through a sieve lined with cheesecloth and set aside. Remove the mussels from their shells and set aside.

Heat a little oil in a deep pan and lightly brown the shallots for several minutes, then add the pumpkin. Pour in the strained cooking liquid from the mussels, add some salt, and bring to a boil. Turn down the heat and simmer gently for about 25 minutes, until the pumpkin is soft. Remove from the heat and blend the soup to a very smooth purée, adding the cream. Add the white wine (if using). Return the soup to the pan, stir in the mussels, reheat, and adjust the seasoning. Serve the soup sprinkled with the chopped parsley, to taste.

### cream of curried pumpkin soup
PREPARATION TIME: 15 MINUTES / COOKING TIME: 30 MINUTES

3 slightly tart apples (such as Granny Smith,
  Golden Delicious, McIntosh)
1 Tbsp (15 mL) curry powder
2 tsp (10 mL) olive oil
1 half-thumb-sized piece of ginger root, peeled,
  and finely chopped
1 onion, peeled and sliced
1 clove garlic, peeled and thinly sliced
2½ lb (1.2 kg) pumpkin (or 1¾ lb/875 g pumpkin flesh),
  peeled, seeded and cut into chunks
3 cups (750 mL) water
salt, freshly ground black pepper

Peel and core the apples, chop into chunks and mix with the curry powder. Heat the oil in a deep pan and lightly brown the ginger, onions, and garlic for several minutes. Then add the pumpkin flesh and apples. Lightly fry for several minutes, then add the measured water and some salt. Allow to simmer for about 25 minutes. When all the ingredients are soft, remove from the heat and set aside some of the cooking water. Blend the soup to a very smooth purée, adding the cooking water, if necessary, to obtain the desired consistency. Reheat and adjust the seasoning to taste.

carrot soups

# carrot soups

## cream of carrot soup

PREPARATION TIME: 10 MINUTES / COOKING TIME: 35 MINUTES

**2 tsp (10 mL) olive oil**
**1 lb (500 g) onions, peeled and sliced**
**1/2 tsp (2mL) ground coriander**
**2 lb (1 kg) carrots, peeled and sliced**
**3 pints (1.5 L) water**
**1/2 cup less 1 Tbsp (100 mL) whipping cream**
**salt, freshly ground black pepper**

Heat the oil in a deep pan and lightly fry the onions with the coriander over very low heat, stirring from time to time, until they are transparent (about 5 minutes). Add the carrots and mix thoroughly. Pour in the measured water and add some salt. Bring to a boil, then turn down the heat and leave to simmer for about 30 minutes. The carrots should be very soft. Remove from the heat and stir in the cream. Blend the soup to a purée and adjust the seasoning.

VARIATION

Add 1 cup (250 mL) of fresh orange juice when blending the soup. Don't add any cream. Pare a few thin strips of orange zest and use to garnish the soup.

# carrot soups

## carrot soup with cilantro
PREPARATION TIME: 10 MINUTES / COOKING TIME: 35 MINUTES

**2 tsp (10 mL) olive oil**
**1 lb (500 g) onions, peeled and sliced**
**1/2 tsp (2 mL) ground coriander**
**2 lb (1 kg) carrots, peeled and sliced**
**3 pints (1.5 L) water**
**1/2 cup less 1 Tbsp (100 mL) whipping cream**
**1 small bunch fresh cilantro, stalks removed, leaves finely chopped**
**salt, freshly ground black pepper**

Heat the oil in a deep pan and lightly fry the onions with the coriander over very low heat, stirring from time to time, until they are transparent (about 5 minutes). Add the carrots and mix thoroughly. Pour in the measured water and add some salt. Bring to a boil, then turn down the heat and leave to simmer for about 30 minutes. The carrots should be very soft. Remove from the heat and add the cream. Blend the soup to a purée, reheat, and adjust the seasoning. Garnish with the chopped cilantro just before serving.

## carrot, citrus, and ginger soup

PREPARATION TIME: 10 MINUTES / COOKING TIME: 35-40 MINUTES

**1 tsp (5 mL) olive oil**
**2 onions, peeled and sliced**
**2 tsp (10 mL) grated fresh ginger (about 1 thumb-sized piece)**
**2 lb (1 kg) carrots, peeled and sliced**
**4 cups (1 L) water**
**3/4 cup (175 mL) orange juice**
**3/4 cup (175 mL) grapefruit juice**
**1 Tbsp (15 mL) lime juice**
**grated rind of 1 lime**
**salt, freshly ground black pepper**

Heat the oil in a deep pan and lightly brown the onions over low to medium heat. Stir in the ginger and continue to cook gently for 5-10 minutes, stirring from time to time. Add the carrots, measured water, and fruit juices, then season with salt, to taste. Bring to a boil, then lower the heat and leave to simmer until the carrots are very soft (about 30 minutes).

Blend the soup to a purée, adding a little water if necessary. Reheat and adjust the seasoning. Serve garnished with the grated lime rind.

TIP
This soup can be served hot or chilled. It will taste even better if you use your own freshly squeezed fruit juice.

# carrot soups

## carrot, celery, and apple soup
PREPARATION TIME: 15 MINUTES / COOKING TIME: 40 MINUTES

**3 large stalks celery**
**2 tsp (10 mL) olive oil**
**2 onions, peeled and sliced**
**1³/₄ lb (875 g) carrots, peeled and cut into rounds**
**3 slightly tart apples (such as Granny Smith, Golden Delicious, McIntosh),**
**peeled, cored, and cut into medium chunks**
**4 cups (1 L) water**
**flat-leaf parsley leaves, for garnish**
**salt, freshly ground black pepper**

Trim the leaves from the celery, remove any stringy parts, then cut into small pieces.
Heat the olive oil in a deep pan and lightly fry the onions and celery over low heat for
10 minutes, stirring from time to time. Add the carrots and apples, then the measured
water along with a little salt.

Bring to a boil, then turn down the heat and leave to simmer for about 30 minutes.
All the vegetables—particularly the carrots—should be very soft. Blend the soup to a
very smooth purée. Serve scattered with flat-leaf parsley leaves.

green soups

# green soups

## nettle soup

PREPARATION TIME: 5 MINUTES / COOKING TIME: 30 MINUTES

1 lb (500 g) young nettle shoots
2 tsp (10 mL) olive oil
2 onions, peeled and sliced
2/3 lb (350 g) potatoes, peeled and diced
4 cups (1 L) water
2/3 cup (150 mL) whipping cream
salt, freshly ground black pepper

Rinse the nettles (wearing gloves to be on the safe side!). Heat the oil in a high-sided pan and lightly brown the onions for about 5 minutes over very low heat. Add the nettles and cover. When the nettles have wilted, add the potatoes and measured water, along with a little salt. Bring to a boil, lower the heat and simmer for 20 minutes. Remove from the heat and blend the soup to a very smooth purée. Adjust the seasoning. Reheat, if necessary and add the cream just before serving.

TIP

The only way to get your hands on some nettles is to pick them yourself, literally. Nettles used for cooking must be young shoots—the ideal time to pick them is during April and May. Don't choose plants taller than 12-16 inches (30-40 cm) and pick only the upper part of the stalk (about 6 inches/15 cm at most). Be careful! Flowering nettles are unfit for consumption! Don't pick nettles near cereal fields, which are likely to have been sprayed with chemicals—nettles from a garden or pasture are ideal. Don't forget to wear gardening or kitchen gloves.

## cauliflower and cumin soup

PREPARATION TIME: 10 MINUTES / COOKING TIME: 20 MINUTES

2 tsp (10 mL) olive oil
1 tsp (5 mL) cumin seeds
1 onion, peeled and sliced
1 lb (500 g) cauliflower, washed and
   broken into florets
2 cups (500 mL) milk
2 cups (500 mL) water
salt, freshly ground black pepper

Heat the oil in a large saucepan and lightly fry the cumin seeds for 1-2 minutes. Add the onion and lightly brown over low heat until it becomes transparent. Add the cauliflower, milk, and water, followed by some salt. Bring to a boil, then turn down the heat and simmer for about 10 minutes. Remove from the heat, blend to a purée, and adjust the seasoning.

## minted pea soup

PREPARATION TIME: 10 MINUTES / COOKING TIME: 35 MINUTES

1 lettuce heart (romaine, butterhead), washed and
   coarsely chopped
3 salad onions or 1 large white onion, peeled and sliced
1 lb (500 g) peas, freshly shelled, or frozen
3 cups (750 mL) water
2 sprigs mint, leaves stripped off
1/2 cup (125 mL) whipping cream
salt

Put the lettuce in a deep pan with the onions and peas. Add the water and a little salt, and bring to a boil. Turn down the heat and simmer for 25 minutes. Remove from the heat, add the cream (setting aside about 1 Tbsp for serving), and the mint leaves. Blend the soup to a very smooth purée. Reheat and adjust the seasoning. Serve with a little swirl of cream on each portion.

VARIATION

This soup can also be served chilled. Delicious on a summer's day!

## cream of garlic soup

PREPARATION TIME: 15 MINUTES / COOKING TIME: 25 MINUTES

**2 large heads garlic**
**2 Tbsp (30 mL) olive oil**
**2 onions, peeled and sliced**
**2/3 lb (350 g) potatoes, peeled, chopped, and rinsed**
**2 cups (500 mL) milk**
**2 cups (500 mL) water**
**salt**

FOR THE CROUTONS
**2 thick slices bread, cut in cubes**
**oil for frying**

Separate, peel, and coarsely chop the garlic cloves. Heat the oil in a large saucepan and lightly fry the garlic over very low heat for several minutes. Add the onions, cook for 3-4 minutes, then add the potatoes. Stir for 1-2 minutes to prevent the potatoes from sticking to the base of the pan. Add the milk and measured water, along with a little salt, and stir all together. Simmer over low heat until the potatoes are soft and well cooked.

In the meantime, heat a little oil in a skillet and fry the cubes of bread on all sides until they are crunchy. Remove from the skillet and drain well on kitchen towels.

Remove the soup from the heat, blend to a very smooth purée, and adjust the seasoning, to taste. Serve in individual bowls with a scattering of croutons.

# green soups

## zucchini and fresh herb soup

PREPARATION TIME: 10 MINUTES / COOKING TIME: 20 MINUTES

**2 lb (1 kg) zucchini, rinsed, trimmed and cut in cubes**
**3 salad onions, peeled and coarsely chopped**
**2 cups (500 mL) water**
**ground cumin**
**2 Tbsp (30 mL) whipping cream**
**2-3 sprigs tarragon, mint, sage or basil**
**salt, freshly ground black pepper**

Put the zucchini and onions in a deep pan. Add the measured water (which should not cover the zucchini, as they have a high water content). Add a large pinch of ground cumin and some salt. Simmer gently until the zucchini are soft (about 15 minutes).

Remove from the heat, add the chosen herbs and the cream. Blend the soup to a purée and adjust the seasoning, to taste.

VARIATION

This creamy soup is also delicious served chilled. In which case, purée the vegetables without adding any cream and leave aside to cool before refrigerating. Thicken by stirring in a cup of plain yogurt, just before serving.

## green-leaf cream soup

PREPARATION TIME: 15 MINUTES / COOKING TIME: 30 MINUTES

**1 lb (500 g) spinach**
**1/4 lb (125 g) sorrel leaves**
**1/4 lb (125 g) dandelion leaves**
**2 tsp (10 mL) olive oil**
**2 shallots, peeled and sliced**
**3 pints (1.5 L) water**
**nutmeg**
**31/2 fl oz (100 mL) whipping cream**
**salt, freshly ground black pepper**

Prepare and wash the spinach, sorrel, and dandelion leaves thoroughly. Heat the oil in a high-sided pan and lightly brown the shallots over low heat for about 5 minutes. Add the greens and fry them lightly for several minutes. Add the measured water and season with salt and pepper. Cover and simmer gently for about 30 minutes. Remove from the heat and add a small grating of nutmeg and the cream. Blend the soup to a very smooth purée and adjust the seasoning, to taste.

VARIATION
You may be able to find dandelion leaves at a farmers' market in the spring. You can leave them out entirely or substitute them with extra sorrel, which may be more readily available, but this will give the soup a slightly sharper flavor. If you pick your own dandelion leaves, avoid roadside verges and anywhere near cereal fields that may have been treated with chemical sprays.

## green cream soup with chorizo

**+ 1 small chorizo sausage (mild or hot, according to taste), sliced**

Fry the slices of chorizo in their own fat in a non-stick skillet. Drain off the dissolved fat and add the chorizo to the soup just before serving.

## green cream soup with poached egg

**+ 1 egg per person**

Boil some water in another saucepan and add a dash of vinegar (2 Tbsps to 4 cups/ 1 L water). Reduce the heat to a simmer, then break an egg into a ladle, lower it into the water and gently slide the egg out. Repeat with the remaining eggs, then remove the saucepan from the heat and allow the eggs to poach for 3 minutes. Remove the eggs and drain them. Place one poached egg in each bowl of soup. Depending on the number of eggs required, it's probably better to poach no more than 2 eggs at a time.

# green soups

## cream of sorrel soup
PREPARATION TIME: 5 MINUTES / COOKING TIME: 25 MINUTES

2 tsp (10 mL) olive oil
3 onions, peeled and sliced
$^2$/3 lb (350 g) potatoes, peeled and chopped
$^3$/4 lb (375 g) sorrel (frozen)
3 cups (750 mL) water
nutmeg
2 Tbsp (30 mL) light cream
salt, freshly ground black pepper

Heat the oil in a deep pan and lightly brown the onions over low heat for 2-3 minutes. Add the potatoes, sorrel, and measured water, followed by some salt, and cook until the sorrel defrosts and the potatoes fall apart (about 20 minutes). Remove from the heat and blend the soup to a very smooth purée. Add a pinch of grated nutmeg and adjust the seasoning, to taste. Reheat if necessary and add a swirl of cream to each bowl just before serving.

## cream of leek soup
PREPARATION TIME: 15 MINUTES / COOKING TIME: 40 MINUTES

2 tsp (10 mL) olive oil
1 onion, peeled and sliced
1$^1$/4 lb (625 g) leeks, thoroughly cleaned and
   finely sliced
1$^1$/2 lb (750 g) potatoes, peeled and diced
4 cups (1 L) water
2 cups (500 mL) milk
1 cup (250 mL) crème fraîche or sour cream
salt, freshly ground black pepper

Heat the oil in a large pan and lightly brown the onion for 5 minutes, then add the leeks. Mix them together and lightly fry for a further 5 minutes. Add the potatoes and measured water, along with a little salt. Cover and simmer gently for 30 minutes, until the vegetables are cooked through. Remove from the heat and blend to a smooth, creamy soup. Add the milk and crème fraîche or sour cream, to obtain the consistency you require. Season to taste and return to the heat for a few more minutes before serving.

## cabbage and meatball soup
PREPARATION TIME: 30 MINUTES / COOKING TIME: 30 MINUTES

FOR THE MEATBALLS
2 Tbsp (30 mL) olive oil
1 small onion, peeled and sliced
1 clove garlic, peeled and sliced
2 slices white sandwich-loaf bread
1 lb (500 g) ground beef or veal
1 egg
1 sprig each thyme and marjoram, leaves stripped
$^1$/4 cup (50 mL) freshly grated Parmesan cheese
salt, freshly ground black pepper

FOR THE SOUP
1 lb (500 g) green cabbage, washed, trimmed,
   (stalk discarded), and chopped into small pieces
olive oil for cooking, if needed
1 large onion, peeled and sliced
1 lb (500 g) tomatoes, washed and chopped
   (to peel, see Tip page 12)
4 cups (1 L) water
salt, freshly ground black pepper

FOR THE MEATBALLS
Heat 1 Tbsp of the oil in a skillet. Lightly soften the onions over very low heat for 2 minutes, then add the sliced garlic. Lightly brown the vegetables for 3-4 minutes then put to one side. Remove the crusts from the bread and reduce the slices to breadcrumbs. In a large bowl, mix together the meat, egg, bread-crumbs, onions and garlic, thyme and marjoram leaves, and the grated Parmesan. Season with salt and pepper to taste. When the mixture is smooth, shape into balls the size of large marbles. Heat the rest of the oil in the skillet and fry the meatballs until golden brown. Put to one side.

FOR THE SOUP
Lightly fry the onions until transparent in the skillet used for the meatballs, adding a little more olive oil if needed, then transfer them to a high-sided pan. Add the cabbage and stir for 1-2 minutes until it has slightly reduced in volume. Add the tomatoes and measured water with a little salt. Bring to a boil, then lower the heat and leave to simmer for a further 15 minutes. Add the meatballs and continue cooking until the cabbage is soft (about 5 minutes). Season to taste.

dried vegetable soups

# dried vegetable soups

## French lentil soup
PREPARATION TIME: 5 MINUTES / COOKING TIME: 15 MINUTES COOKING TIME

**2 Tbsp (30 mL) olive oil**
**2 onions, peeled and sliced**
**1 lb (500 g) French (Puy) lentils, rinsed**
**4 pints (2 L) water**
**1 Tbsp (15 mL) lemon juice**
**salt, freshly ground black pepper**

Heat 1 Tbsp of the olive oil in a deep pan and lightly fry the onions over low heat, until they are transparent. Add the lentils and measured water, along with a little salt. Simmer gently for 45 minutes, stirring occasionally, until the lentils are cooked through. Stir in the lemon juice and the remaining olive oil. Blend the soup to a purée and adjust the seasoning.

VARIATION
Add the coarsely chopped leaves of a small bunch of cilantro or stir in 2 tsp (10 mL) of curry powder when browning the onions.

## French lentil and bacon soup
PREPARATION TIME: 5 MINUTES / COOKING TIME: 55 MINUTES

**2 Tbsp (30 mL) olive oil, plus a little extra**
**2 onions, peeled and sliced**
**1 lb (500 g) French (Puy) lentils, rinsed**
**3 slices smoked bacon, finely diced**
**4 pints (2 L) water**
**salt, freshly ground black pepper**

Heat 1 Tbsp of olive oil in a deep pan and lightly fry the onions over low heat. When the onions are transparent, add the lentils, 1/3 of the diced bacon, and the measured water. Add a little salt and simmer gently until the lentils are cooked through (about 45 minutes), stirring occasionally. Stir in the lemon juice and the remaining olive oil. Blend the soup to a smooth purée and adjust the seasoning, to taste.

To serve, fry the rest of the bacon in a little oil until golden brown and add to the soup just before serving.

## French lentil and sausage soup
PREPARATION TIME: 10 MINUTES / COOKING TIME: 50 MINUTES

**1 tsp (5 mL) olive oil**
**1 onion, peeled and sliced**
**1 carrot, peeled and sliced**
**3/4 lb (400 g) French (Puy) lentils, rinsed**
**4 pints (2 L) water**
**1 bouquet garni**
**1 Morteau sausage, or other smoked pork sausage**
**salt, freshly ground black pepper**

Heat the olive oil in a deep pan and lightly brown the onion, stirring from time to time. Add the carrots and lentils and stir all these ingredients together. Pour in the measured water, add the bouquet garni and the whole sausage. Add a little salt. Bring to a boil, then lower the heat and simmer for at least 45 minutes, stirring occasionally.

When the lentils are thoroughly cooked, remove the bouquet garni and the sausage. Put the sausage to one side. Blend the lentil soup thoroughly to obtain a really smooth consistency. Peel the Morteau sausage and cut into slices, then quarter each slice. Reheat the soup, seasoning to taste, and add the pieces of sausage.

# dried vegetable soups

## Indian-style lentil soup
PREPARATION TIME: 5 MINUTES / COOKING TIME: 55 MINUTES

2 Tbsp (30 mL) olive oil
1 onion, peeled and sliced
2 Tbsp (30 mL) ground coriander
2 tsp (10 mL) ground cumin
2 tsp (10 mL) grated fresh ginger (about 1 thumb-sized piece)
1 lb (500 g) yellow lentils, rinsed
4 pints (2 L) water
1/2 lb (250 g) peeled tomatoes (to peel, see Tip on page 12)
   or 1 x 8-oz/250-g can
1 Tbsp (15 mL) fresh lime juice, or to taste
fresh mint or cilantro leaves, shredded
salt, freshly ground black pepper

Heat the oil in a deep pan and lightly fry the onion until it becomes transparent (about 5 minutes). Add the spices and ginger and lightly fry for several minutes. Lower the heat and add the lentils. Mix well, then gradually pour in the measured water, stirring regularly. Add a little salt.

Bring to a boil, then turn down the heat and simmer until the lentils are cooked through (30-45 minutes), stirring occasionally. Add the tomatoes and lime juice, and cook for another 5 minutes. Remove from the heat and blend the soup to a purée. Adjust the seasoning to taste. Serve the soup garnished with the shredded fresh mint or cilantro leaves.

## French lentil soup with fresh mussels
PREPARATION TIME: 15 MINUTES / COOKING TIME: 50 MINUTES

1 quart (1 L) mussels
3/4 cup (175 mL) white wine
4 shallots, peeled and sliced
4 cups (1 L) water
3/4 lb (400 g) French (Puy) lentils, rinsed
salt, freshly ground black pepper

Wash and scrub the mussels thoroughly, removing the "beards." Put the white wine, shallots, and mussels in a large, deep pan. Cover and cook over high heat for 5 minutes. Season with salt and pepper, turn down the heat and simmer for another 5 minutes.

Lift the mussels from the pan with a slotted spoon, discarding any that have not opened, and reserve the cooking liquid after straining it through a sieve lined with cheesecloth. Remove the mussels from the shells and keep warm. Pour the measured water into the deep pan along with the strained cooking liquid, add the lentils, and simmer for about 35-40 minutes, stirring occasionally, until the lentils are very soft. Remove from the heat and blend the soup thoroughly to obtain a smooth consistency. Adjust the seasoning to taste. Reheat the soup and add the warm mussels just before serving.

## red lentil, lime, and coconut soup
PREPARATION TIME: 5 MINUTES / COOKING TIME: 50 MINUTES

1 Tbsp (15 mL) olive oil
2 onions, peeled and sliced
2 cloves garlic, peeled and sliced
2 tsp (10 mL) ground cumin
1/2 tsp (2 mL) ground cinnamon
3/4 lb (375 g) red lentils
1 x 28-oz (800-g) can peeled tomatoes
4 pints (2 L) water
3/4 cup plus 2 Tbsp (200 mL) coconut milk
1 Tbsp (15 mL) fresh lime juice, or to taste
salt, freshly ground black pepper

Heat the olive oil in a deep pan and lightly brown the onions and garlic with the spices for 5 minutes over low heat. Add the lentils and tomatoes. Stir well and pour in the measured water. Stir again and season with salt and pepper to taste.

Leave to simmer until the lentils are cooked through (about 45 minutes), stirring occasionally. Remove from the heat, add the coconut milk and lime juice. Blend the soup to a very smooth purée. Adjust the seasoning, to taste, before serving.

# dried vegetable soups

## white bean and chorizo soup
PREPARATION TIME: 10 MINUTES / COOKING TIME: 1¹/₄ HOURS

**2 tsp (10 mL) olive oil plus a little extra**
**2 onions, peeled and finely diced**
**2 carrots, peeled and finely diced**
**1 small leek, thoroughly cleaned, trimmed, and finely chopped**
**2 cloves garlic, peeled and finely diced**
**5 pints (2.5 L) water**
**³/₄ lb (375 g) dried white navy beans, rinsed**
**1 sprig thyme**
**1 chorizo (mild or hot, according to taste)**
**salt, freshly ground black pepper**

Heat the oil in a large, deep pan, add the onions, carrots, leek, and garlic, and soften over medium heat for about 5 minutes. Add the beans and the measured water and bring to a boil over high heat. Skim off any scum with a slotted spoon. Lower the heat and simmer for about an hour until the beans become soft, but not too soft. Don't allow the simmering to get too strong or the abrasion will loosen the bean skins and they'll lose their form. Only add salt toward the end of the cooking time, otherwise it will prevent the beans from softening.

In the meantime, cut the chorizo into slices and lightly fry them in a little olive oil in a skillet over low heat. Set aside and keep warm.

Remove the soup from the heat, ladle half into a blender and purée to a smooth consistency. Return the purée to the pan and stir in the remaining unblended soup. Reheat and adjust the seasoning to taste. Add the chorizo slices just before serving.

## chili bean and tomato soup

PREPARATION TIME: 10 MINUTES / COOKING TIME: 35 MINUTES

**1 lb (500 g) very ripe tomatoes, peeled (see page 12)**
**and chopped or 1 x 16-oz/500-g can tomatoes**
**1 lb (500 g) canned kidney beans, drained and rinsed**
**2 cups (500 mL) water**
**2 cloves garlic, peeled and crushed**
**2 Tbsp(30 mL) lemon juice**
**2 tsp (10 mL) chili paste**
**salt**

Put the tomatoes and kidney beans in a large, deep pan. Add the measured water and garlic, along with a little salt. Cover and simmer gently for at least 30 minutes.

Remove from the heat when the kidney beans are cooked through. Add the lemon juice, chili paste, and a little water, if necessary. Blend the soup to a coarse purée and check the seasoning.

## fava bean and cumin soup

PREPARATION TIME: 5 MINUTES / COOKING TIME: 40 MINUTES

3 Tbsp (45 mL) olive oil
2 onions, peeled and sliced
4 cloves garlic, peeled and sliced
1 tsp (5 mL) ground cumin
2/3 lb (350 g) small dried fava beans
4 pints (2 L) water
1 Tbsp (15 mL) lemon juice
1 tsp (5 mL) cumin seeds
salt, freshly ground black pepper

Heat 1 Tbsp of the oil in a large, deep pan and lightly brown the onions and garlic for 5 minutes with the ground cumin. Add the fava beans and the measured water. Bring to a boil, then simmer gently until the fava beans are soft (about 30 minutes), adding a little salt toward the end of the cooking time. Remove from the heat, stir in the lemon juice and the rest of the olive oil. Blend to a very smooth purée and add the cumin seeds. Check the seasoning before serving.

## split pea and bacon soup

PREPARATION TIME: 10 MINUTES / COOKING TIME: 45 MINUTES

1 Tbsp (15 mL) olive oil
1 onion, peeled and thinly sliced
1/2 lb (250 g) leeks, outer leaves removed, rinsed
  and thinly sliced
2 cups (500 mL) water
1/2 lb (250 g) split peas, rinsed in cold water
1/4 lb (125 g) carrots, peeled and diced
1 sprig thyme,
1 sprig bay
2 strips smoked bacon, diced
salt, freshly ground black pepper

Heat the olive oil in a deep pan and lightly brown the onion and leeks for 5 minutes. Add the measured water, split peas, carrots, thyme, and bay (tie the thyme and bay together with string and fasten the other end to the pan handle for easy removal). Add a little salt and pepper, cover, and allow to cook for 30-40 minutes over low heat.

In the meantime, lightly brown the diced bacon in its own fat in a skillet. Put to one side. When the split peas are soft, remove the thyme and bay sprigs and blend the soup to a very smooth purée. Adjust the seasoning and add the bacon. Serve piping hot.

## oriental chickpea soup

PREPARATION TIME: 15 MINUTES / COOKING TIME: 35 MINUTES

2 tsp (10 mL) olive oil
1 tsp (5 mL) curry powder
1 tsp (5 mL) ground cumin
2 cloves garlic, peeled and sliced
1 onion, peeled and sliced
2/3 lb (350 g) tomatoes, peeled (see page 12), and
  chopped, or 1 1/2 cups (350 mL) canned tomatoes
1 x 1/2-lb (250-g) can chickpeas, rinsed and drained
1 bunch flat-leaf parsley, washed and stalks removed
2 cups (500 mL) water
1 handful raisins
salt, freshly ground black pepper

Heat the olive oil in a deep pan and lightly fry the spices. Add the garlic and onion and lightly brown for 5 minutes over low heat, stirring continuously. Add the tomatoes, chickpeas, and parsley. Pour in the measured water and add a little salt.

Cover and simmer gently for about 30 minutes. Remove from the heat and blend to a purée. Add the raisins just before serving.

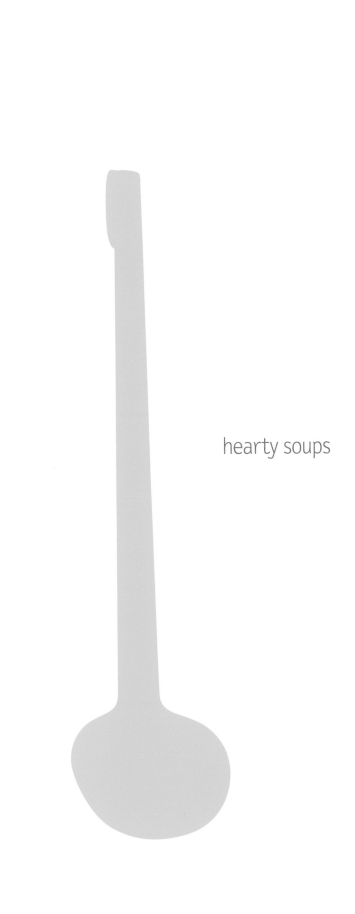

hearty soups

## farmers' market vegetable soup

PREPARATION TIME: 10 MINUTES / COOKING TIME: 30 MINUTES

**1 large carrot or 2 medium carrots, peeled and thinly sliced**
**1 leek, washed, trimmed, and thinly sliced**
**¼ cabbage (green or white), washed and thinly sliced**
**1 onion, peeled and thinly sliced**
**4-5 lettuce leaves, washed and shredded**
**1 turnip, peeled and thinly sliced**
**salt, freshly ground black pepper**

This delicious vegetable soup is often featured in the spring issues of women's magazines as a "fat-busting" soup. Although made without potatoes or fat, it tastes great and is very filling.

Put all the vegetables in a deep pan. Cover with water and add a little salt and pepper. Leave to simmer over moderate heat for 20-30 minutes, until all the vegetables are very soft (particularly the carrots). Either serve the soup as it is or blend it into a coarse purée for a smoother consistency.

SUMMER VARIATION
Substitute the cabbage and turnip for a sliced zucchini and a tomato.

# hearty soups

## two celeries and chicken soup
PREPARATION TIME: 20 MINUTES / COOKING TIME: 45 MINUTES

**4 stalks celery**
**2 Tbsp (30 mL) olive oil plus a little extra**
**1 lb (500 g) potatoes, peeled and finely diced**
**1 celeriac (celery root), peeled and finely diced**
**5 cups (1.2 L) water**
**2 skinless chicken breasts**
**salt, freshly ground black pepper**

Remove any stringy parts from the celery and cut the stalks into small chunks.
Heat the olive oil in a large, deep pan and lightly brown the celery over very low heat
for about 10 minutes. Add the potato and celeriac, along with the measured water
and a little salt. Simmer gently until the potatoes fall apart (about 30-40 minutes).
In the meantime, thinly slice the chicken breasts and lightly fry the pieces in a little oil
until golden brown. Season with salt and pepper and put to one side. Blend the soup
to a coarse purée, adjust the seasoning, to taste, and add the chicken pieces just
before serving.

## Portuguese smoked haddock soup
PREPARATION TIME: 20 MINUTES / COOKING TIME: 30 MINUTES

**1¹/₂ lb (800 g) Portuguese cabbage (or curly kale)**
**5 cups (1.2 L) water**
**1 lb (500 g) potatoes, peeled and cut into pieces**
**2 cloves garlic, peeled and crushed**
**¹/₂ lb (250 g) carrots, peeled and diced**
**1 fillet smoked haddock**
**salt, freshly ground black pepper**

Remove and discard the outer leaves and the stalks
of the cabbage and shred the fresh leaves. Pour the
measured water into a deep pan and add the potatoes
and garlic along with a little salt. Bring to a boil, then
turn down the heat, add the cabbage and carrots, and
continue cooking for 20-25 minutes. The potatoes
should fall apart and the carrots should be very soft.

Remove from the heat and blend the soup to a coarse
purée. Don't add too much salt or pepper, as the soup
will acquire a smoky, salty flavor from the haddock.
Skin the haddock and slice the fillet into small pieces,
taking care to remove any stray bones. Add the pieces
of smoked fish just before serving.

### VARIATION
Substitute the haddock with a small chorizo sausage.
Slice the chorizo and fry it quickly in its own fat in a
non-stick skillet over high heat. Remove from the pan,
drain on kitchen towels, and add to the soup just
before serving.

## borscht
PREPARATION TIME: 15 MINUTES / COOKING TIME: 35 MINUTES

**1 Tbsp (15 mL) olive oil**
**2 leeks, washed, outer leaves removed if damaged,**
  **and sliced**
**2 carrots, peeled and sliced**
**2 potatoes, peeled and cut into pieces**
**2 red beets, peeled and cut into pieces**
**¹/₂ red cabbage, washed and trimmed, stalk discarded**
**1 onion, peeled and sliced**
**2 tomatoes, peeled (see page 12) and chopped,**
  **or 8 oz (250 g) canned tomatoes**
**red wine vinegar**
**¹/₂-1 cup (125-250 mL) sour cream**
**salt, freshly ground black pepper**

Heat the olive oil in a deep pan and fry the onion
and leeks lightly for 5 minutes over low heat, until
transparent. Then add the rest of the vegetables,
and water, which should not completely cover the
vegetables. Season with salt and pepper. Cover and
simmer for 30 minutes, stirring from time to time.
When the vegetables are well cooked, blend to a
coarse purée. Add a dash of red wine vinegar and
adjust the seasoning, to taste. Serve with the sour
cream separately for people to help themselves.

# hearty soups

## corn and red bell pepper soup
PREPARATION TIME: 5 MINUTES / COOKING TIME: 30 MINUTES

1 Tbsp (15 mL) olive oil
1 onion, peeled and sliced
1 sprig thyme, leaves stripped
1 stalk celery, trimmed and chopped
1/2 red bell pepper, peeled (see Tip below) and sliced
3/4 lb (375 g) canned corn
1 cup (250 mL) water
1 cup (250 mL) milk
salt, freshly ground black pepper

Heat a little oil in a high-sided cooking pot and lightly brown the onion and thyme leaves for about 5 minutes, then add the celery. Mix with the onion and allow to brown for 5 minutes. Add the red bell pepper, mix well, and brown for a further 5 minutes, then add the corn along with the water. Season with salt and pepper. Bring to a boil, then turn down the heat, cover, and simmer gently for 10 minutes.

Remove from the heat, add the milk, and blend just long enough to obtain a very creamy, purée consistency. Adjust the seasoning, to taste.

In Argentina, this soup is known as *mazamorra* and the vegetables are not puréed.

TIP
To peel bell peppers, roast in a hot oven or under a broiler until the skins blacken and blister. Put in a plastic bag, sealed, for about 15-20 minutes, where their own steam will help to loosen the skins.

# hearty soups

## chestnut and bacon soup

PREPARATION TIME: 15 MINUTES / COOKING TIME: 45 MINUTES

**2 tsp (10 mL) olive oil**
**1 carrot, peeled and sliced into rounds**
**1 onion, peeled and sliced**
**1 stalk celery stick, washed, trimmed and sliced**
**2 cloves garlic, peeled and sliced**
**1¼ lb (625 g) canned chestnuts, rinsed**
**1 bouquet garni (parsley, thyme, bay ... tied into a bunch)**
**3 pints (1.5 L) water**
**³/4 lb (375 g) smoked bacon, finely diced**
**salt, freshly ground black pepper**

Heat the oil in a deep pan and lightly fry all the vegetables for about 5 minutes over low heat, stirring from time to time. Add the chestnuts, the bouquet garni, and the measured water. Season with salt and pepper and bring to a boil. Turn down the heat, cover, and simmer for 40 minutes.

When the chestnuts are cooked through, remove from the heat and take out the bouquet garni. Blend the soup to a very smooth purée. Adjust the seasoning, to taste but without adding too much salt, as the bacon will make the soup quite salty. Lightly brown the diced bacon in its own fat in a very hot non-stick skillet, drain on kitchen towels, and add to the soup just before serving.

## French onion soup

PREPARATION TIME: 15 MINUTES / COOKING TIME: 50 MINUTES

**2 tsp (10 mL) olive oil**
**8 onions, peeled and sliced**
**1 clove garlic, crushed**
**2 Tbsp (30 mL) all-purpose flour**
**³/4 cup (200 mL) white wine**
**3 pints (1.5 L) poultry stock, or**
**   use 2 chicken stock cubes**
**1 sprig thyme, leaves stripped**
**6-12 slices white bread**
**½ cup (125 mL) grated Gruyère cheese**
**salt, freshly ground black pepper**

Heat the olive oil in a large, deep pan and fry the onions for 20 minutes, stirring frequently, until they turn a deep golden brown. Add the garlic and flour, stirring continuously for 1-2 minutes. Pour in the white wine and stir until the flour is fully absorbed. Gently bring to a boil, stirring continuously, then gradually pour in the stock. Bring back to a boil, add the thyme leaves, season with salt and pepper, and leave to simmer for 20 minutes.

Just before serving, toast the bread, making a slice for each bowl, sprinkle with grated cheese and brown under the broiler. You can also put the bread at the bottom of the soup bowls, pour the soup over it, and sprinkle with the grated cheese, which will melt.

## Provençal soup

PREPARATION TIME: 15 MINUTES / COOKING TIME: 30 MINUTES

**1 Tbsp (15 mL) olive oil**
**1 red bell pepper, seeded, and finely diced**
**4 cloves garlic, peeled and sliced**
**4 shallots, peeled and thinly sliced**
**1 eggplant, rinsed, peeled and diced**
**2 zucchini, rinsed, trimmed, and sliced**
**½ lb (250 g) tomatoes, chopped**
**1 sprig thyme**
**2 bay leaves**
**4 cups (1 L) water**
**1 sprig basil, leaves stripped**
**1 Tbsp (15 mL) lemon juice**
**salt, freshly ground black pepper**

Heat the oil in a deep pan and lightly fry the bell pepper, garlic, and shallots for several minutes. Add the eggplant, zucchini, tomatoes, thyme sprig, bay leaves, and measured water. Season with salt and pepper. Bring to a boil, then leave to cook over low heat until all the vegetables are soft (about 15-20 minutes).

Remove the thyme and bay leaves, then add the basil leaves and lemon juice. Blend the soup to a purée. Adjust the seasoning, to taste, before serving.

# hearty soups

## green cabbage and shallot soup
PREPARATION TIME: 10 MINUTES / COOKING TIME: 40 MINUTES

1 Tbsp (15 mL) olive oil
5 oz (150 g) shallots, peeled and sliced
3 Tbsp (45 mL) vinegar
1/2 green cabbage, washed, trimmed, and finely shredded
3/4 lb (375 g) potatoes, peeled, and diced
5 cups (1.25 L) water
salt, freshly ground black pepper

Heat the olive oil in a skillet and lightly brown the shallots. As soon as they turn an attractive golden color, add the vinegar to deglaze the skillet. Put aside about 1/3 of the shallots and transfer the rest to a deep pan. Add the cabbage and potatoes and cover with the measured water. Season with salt and pepper. Cover, and simmer over a medium heat until the vegetables are very well cooked (about 20-25 minutes). Blend to a coarse purée. Garnish with the remaining shallots just before serving.

## thick vegetable and meat broth (*garbure*)
PREPARATION TIME: 25 MINUTES / COOKING TIME: 1³/4 HOURS

1 lb (500 g) dried white navy beans
6¹/2 pints (3 L) water
2 lb (1 kg) potatoes, peeled and cut in small dice
5 carrots, peeled and cut in small dice
1 large leek or 2 small leeks, trimmed and finely sliced
1 cured ham hock
1 Tbsp (15 mL) duck or goose fat
2 onions, peeled and sliced
1 small green cabbage, washed, trimmed and shredded
6 pieces duck, goose, or pork confit (fresh or canned)
1/2 tsp (2 mL) chili powder
salt, freshly ground black pepper

Put the beans in a high-sided cooking pot and pour in the measured water. Bring to a boil over high heat and skim off any scum with a slotted spoon. Lower the heat to moderate and add the potatoes, carrots, leek, ham hock, and chili powder. Cover, and cook for 30 minutes, skimming if necessary.

In the meantime, heat the duck or goose fat in a skillet and lightly brown the onions for about 5 minutes. Put to one side.

After the soup has been cooking for 30 minutes, add the cabbage and onions, and cook for a about 1 hour. The beans should be soft and the soup thoroughly cooked and very thick. Heat the confit. Add to the soup 10 minutes before serving. Serve piping hot with chunks of rustic bread.

Like all traditional regional recipes, there are probably a great many takes on the recipe for a *garbure*: some people add garlic, others don't, some people substitute bacon or salted belly pork for the ham, etc. However, all agree that *garbure* is an extremely thick soup (the spoon should stand up by itself!) and that duck or goose fat is a must.

## vegetable soup with *pistou*
PREPARATION TIME: 25 MINUTES / COOKING TIME: 35 MINUTES

FOR THE *PISTOU*
5 cloves garlic, peeled and crushed
3 large basil sprigs, washed and leaves stripped
1/2 cup (125 mL) olive oil

FOR THE SOUP
1 Tbsp (15 mL) olive oil
2 onions, peeled and finely chopped
1 leek, washed, trimmed, and finely sliced
2 cloves garlic, peeled and finely chopped
1 carrot, peeled and finely chopped
3 ripe tomatoes, peeled (see page 12) and finely chopped
1 zucchini, washed, trimmed, and finely chopped
2 potatoes, peeled and finely chopped
2 handfuls green beans
2 handfuls white beans
3 pints (1.5 L) water
4 oz (125 g) pasta shells or small pasta shapes
2 handfuls fresh fava beans
1 cup (250 mL) freshly grated Parmesan cheese
salt, freshly ground black pepper

To make the *pistou*, purée the garlic and basil leaves in a blender, gradually adding the olive oil to obtain a creamy consistency. Chill in the refrigerator.

To make the soup, heat the oil in a deep pan and lightly fry the onions, leek, and garlic for 5 minutes. Add the rest of the vegetables (except the fava beans, which are added after the soup is cooked) and the measured water. Season lightly with salt and pepper.

Bring to a boil and add the pasta. Cover and simmer for 20 minutes over medium heat. Add the fava beans and cook for 2 minutes. Adjust the seasoning, to taste. Serve piping hot, adding a large spoonful of *pistou* to each bowl. Hand round a bowl of grated Parmesan.

cheese soups

# cheese soups

## zucchini and cheese soup

PREPARATION TIME: 5 MINUTES / 15 MINUTES COOKING TIME

2 lb (1 kg) zucchini, washed, trimmed and sliced
4 salad onions, washed and coarsely chopped
2 cups (500 mL) water
ground cumin
4 portions Kiri or 3 oz (80 g) other cream cheese
salt

Put the zucchini and onions in a deep pan, add a large pinch of ground cumin, salt, and the measured water, which should not completely cover the vegetables. Cook over low heat until the zucchini are soft (about 15 minutes). Remove from the heat. Ladle out about a cup of the cooking liquid and set it aside in case you need to thin the soup, although zucchini have a fairly high water content and may actually release water while cooking.

Add the Kiri portions and blend the soup to a very smooth purée. If the soup is a little too thick, thin down with all or part of the reserved cooking liquid. Adjust the seasoning, to taste.

Using Kiri instead of crème fraîche or sour cream adds a delicate flavor to the soup. You can also use Boursin cheese, which results in a slightly garlicky flavor.

## broccoli and cheese soup

PREPARATION TIME: 10 MINUTES / COOKING TIME: 30 MINUTES

3/4 lb (375 g) broccoli, washed and separated
   into florets
1/4 lb (125 g) carrots, peeled and finely chopped
1/2 lb (250 g) potatoes, peeled and finely chopped
1/4 lb (125 g) shallots, peeled and sliced
4 cups (1 L) water
10 portions Laughing Cow cheese
salt, freshly ground black pepper

Put the vegetables in a deep pan with the measured water. Season with salt and pepper. Cover, and cook over medium heat for about 30 minutes. All the vegetables should be cooked through. Remove from the heat, add the cheese portions and blend the soup to a smooth purée. Adjust the seasoning, to taste.

## celery and blue cheese soup

PREPARATION TIME: 10 MINUTES / COOKING TIME: 35 MINUTES

2 tsp (10 mL) olive oil
2 onions, peeled and sliced
1 celeriac (celery root), peeled and chopped
4 cups (1 L) water
1/4 lb (125 g) creamy, soft blue cheese,
Bleu d'Auvergne if possible
salt, freshly ground black pepper
croutons (optional, see recipe on page 46)

Heat a little olive oil in a skillet and add the onions. Cover, and fry over low heat until they become transparent, stirring from time to time. Add the celeriac and measured water, along with a little salt. Cover and bring to a boil, then turn down the heat and leave to simmer until the celeriac is very soft (about 25 minutes). Remove from the heat and add 3/4 of the cheese.

Blend the soup to a very smooth purée and adjust the seasoning, to taste. Cut the rest of the cheese into very small pieces and add them to the soup just before serving. This soup is particularly delicious garnished with croutons.

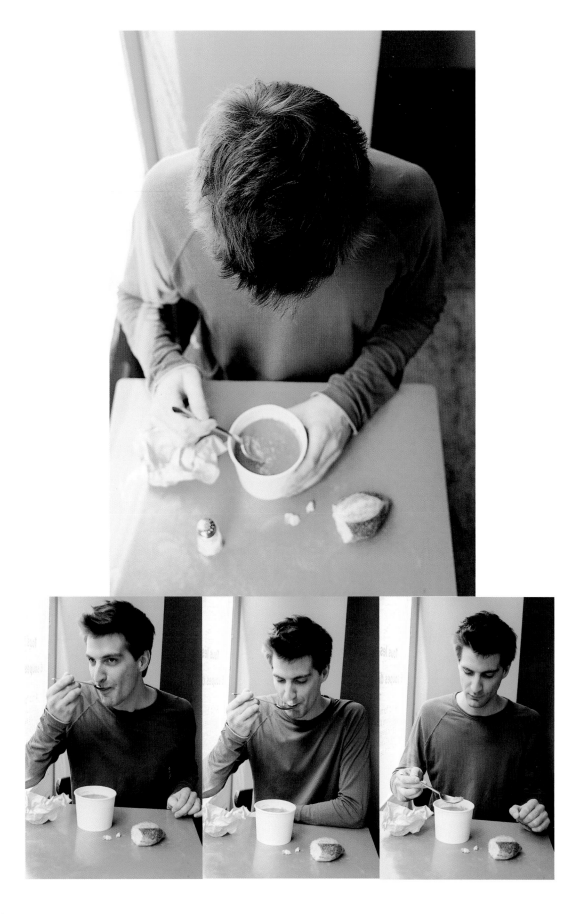

# cheese soups

## tomato, apple, and ricotta soup

PREPARATION TIME: 10 MINUTES / COOKING TIME: 30 MINUTES

1 tsp (5 mL) olive oil
1 onion, peeled and sliced
4 apples (such as Golden Delicious, McIntosh ...)
4$^1$/2 lb (2 kg) very ripe tomatoes, peeled (see page 12), seeded
   and chopped (or 2 x 28 oz cans and 1 x 16 oz can tomatoes)
4 cups (1 L) water
$^1$/4 cup (50 ml) ricotta
1 Tbsp (15 mL) tomato paste
salt, freshly ground black pepper

Heat the olive oil in a large, high-sided pan and lightly brown the onion over low heat. In the meantime, peel and chop the apples, then add them with the tomatoes to the onion. Pour in the measured water followed by the tomato paste, mixing well. Add some salt. Bring to a boil, then reduce to low heat and allow to simmer for about 20 minutes.

Remove from the heat, add the ricotta, and blend the soup to a smooth purée. Adjust the seasoning to taste, before serving.

# cheese soups

## white Parmesan soup

PREPARATION TIME: 10 MINUTES / COOKING TIME: 10 MINUTES

**7 oz (200 g) Parmesan cheese**
**1/2 lb (250 g) stale sandwich bread (about 8 slices), crusts removed**
**4 pints (2 L) poultry stock, or use 3 stock cubes**
**salt, freshly ground black pepper**

Finely grate 3/4 of the Parmesan, leaving the remaining cheese aside in one piece.
Cut the bread into large pieces and put through a blender to make very fine
breadcrumbs. Mix the breadcrumbs thoroughly with the grated cheese to obtain
an even mixture.

Bring the stock to a boil in a deep pan, then reduce to low heat, and gradually add
the bread and cheese mix, whisking gently from time to time to loosen it. Cook gently
for about 5 minutes. The soup should be creamy like a fondue—not too thick or runny.
Add a little freshly ground black pepper, and salt to taste, but remember that the
cheese will add a salty flavor.

Shave curls of cheese from the reserved piece of Parmesan and use to garnish the
soup just before serving. Don't prepare the shavings too long before using as the
cheese will dry out.

Gazpacho

Velouté glacé de courges

Bloody Mary

Soupe froide de pe...

Soupe du marché

soups to impress

# soups to impress

## bloody mary

PREPARATION TIME: 10 MINUTES / COOKING TIME: 30 MINUTES

4 stalks celery, washed, trimmed and finely chopped
2 tsp (10 mL) olive oil
3 lb (1.5 kg) very ripe tomatoes, peeled (see page 12) and chopped
   (or 3 x 16-oz/500-g cans tomatoes)
2 limes
$\frac{1}{2}$ cup less 1 Tbsp (100 mL) vodka
1 Tbsp (15 mL) Tabasco
1 Tbsp (15 mL) Worcestershire sauce
salt, freshly ground black pepper

Heat the olive oil in a deep pan and lightly brown the celery over low heat for about
15 minutes, stirring from time to time, until it becomes soft. Add the tomatoes
and the grated rind of $\frac{1}{2}$ a lime. Add some salt, cover, and simmer for 10 minutes.
Remove from the heat and blend the soup to a very smooth purée.

Add the vodka and the juice of both limes, or to taste, and the Tabasco and
Worcestershire sauces. You can vary the amount of vodka and Tabasco you use
according to individual taste. Adjust the seasoning before serving.

VARIATION
This soup is just as delicious served chilled with a couple of ice cubes in each bowl.

# soups to impress

## creamy leek and orange soup
PREPARATION TIME: 15 MINUTES / COOKING TIME: 30 MINUTES

1 Tbsp (15 mL) olive oil
1/4 lb (125 g) onions, peeled and chopped
1 lb (500 g) leeks (white part only), trimmed and sliced
1/2 lb (250 g) potatoes, peeled and diced
4 cups (1 L) water
1 orange
1 1/3 cups (300 mL) whipping cream
1 Tbsp (15 mL) Cointreau
salt

Heat the olive oil in a deep pan and lightly fry the onions and leeks over low heat for 5 minutes, stirring from time to time. Add the potatoes and measured water, along with a little salt. Bring to a boil, then turn down the heat and leave to simmer for 20 minutes.

In the meantime, scrub the orange thoroughly, and grate most of the rind, paring the rest into thin strips with a zester or very sharp knife. Mix the grated rind with 1/2 of the cream and the Cointreau, and chill in the refrigerator. When the vegetables are cooked through, remove the pan from the heat and add the remaining cream. Blend the soup to a very smooth purée. Just before serving, lightly whip the orange-flavored cream and pour it over the soup. Garnish with the strips of orange zest.

## pumpkin and avocado soup
PREPARATION TIME: 15 MINUTES / COOKING TIME: 30 MINUTES

2 tsp (10 mL) olive oil
2 onions, peeled and sliced
1 clove garlic, peeled and crushed
2 lb (1 kg) pumpkin flesh, seeded and chopped
3 cups (750 mL) water
1 or 2 large ripe avocados
nutmeg
Tabasco (optional)
salt, freshly ground black pepper

Heat the oil in a deep pan and lightly brown the onions and garlic for about 5 minutes, stirring from time to time. Add the pumpkin and measured water, along with a little salt. Bring to a boil, then turn down the heat and leave to simmer until the pumpkin is very soft. Remove from the heat and take out a ladle or two of cooking liquid and set aside.

Blend the soup, adding a little of reserved cooking liquid if you need to thin the soup to the desired consistency. Grate in nutmeg to taste and check the seasoning. Peel the avocado, discard the pit, and chop the flesh into small cubes. Add the avocado to the soup and season liberally with ground black pepper or a few drops of Tabasco (if using), according to taste.

## carrot, pineapple, and ginger soup
PREPARATION TIME: 15 MINUTES / COOKING TIME: 40 MINUTES

1 tsp (5 mL) olive oil
2 onions, peeled and sliced
2 tsp (10 mL) grated fresh ginger
   (about 1 thumb-sized piece)
1 lb (500 g) carrots, peeled and sliced
4 cups (1 L) water
3/4 cup (175 mL) pineapple juice
1/2 fresh pineapple, peeled and cut into pieces or
1 can pineapple
salt, freshly ground black pepper

Heat the oil in a deep pan and lightly brown the onions, stirring from time to time. Add the ginger and brown for several minutes. Then add the carrots, measured water, and pineapple juice. Season with salt.

Bring to a boil, then turn down the heat and leave to simmer for about 30 minutes, or until the carrots are really soft. Add the pineapple and blend the soup to a purée, adding a little water if necessary. Adjust the seasoning, to taste.

VARIATION
This soup can be served hot or chilled.

# soups to impress

## curried celery and mussel soup

PREPARATION TIME: 20 MINUTES / COOKING TIME: 50 MINUTES

1 quart (1 L) mussels
4 cups (1 L) water
2 tsp (10 mL) olive oil
1 lb (500 g) stalks celery, scrubbed, trimmed, and finely sliced
3/4 lb (375 g) potatoes, peeled and chopped
1 tsp (5mL) curry powder
3/4 cup (175 mL) whipping cream
salt, freshly ground black pepper
celery leaves, for garnish

Rinse the mussels in running water to remove any sand or grit. Scrub the shells thoroughly, removing the "beards," and put them in a large saucepan with the measured water and a little salt. Cook over moderate heat until they open—make sure you discard any that remain closed. Remove the mussels from the shells and leave to one side. Strain the cooking liquid through a sieve lined with cheesecloth and set aside.

Heat the oil in a deep pan and lightly brown the celery for 10-15 minutes, stirring frequently. Add the potatoes, curry powder, a little salt, and some of the cooking liquid from the mussels. Simmer gently for about 30 minutes, topping up with the remaining cooking liquid when necessary. Remove from the heat, blend the soup to a purée and adjust the seasoning, to taste. Thicken the soup with the cream and add the mussels. Serve piping hot garnished with the celery leaves.

broths and stocks

# broths and stocks

## poultry stock

PREPARATION TIME: 10 MINUTES / 2-3 HOURS COOKING TIME

1 onion
1 carrot
1 stalk celery
1 leek
1 or 2 poultry carcasses (chicken, duck, guinea fowl, etc.)
6½ pints (3 L) water
1 bouquet garni (1 or 2 sprigs thyme and 1 bay leaf, rolled
   in a green leek leaf and tied firmly with string)
salt, freshly ground black pepper

Peel and/or trim and coarsely chop all the vegetables, then put in a high-sided stockpot along with the carcass. Cover with the measured water, add the bouquet garni, and season sparingly with salt and pepper. Bring to a boil, skim off any scum with a slotted spoon, reduce the heat and leave to simmer for 2-3 hours. Skim the surface regularly. The longer the broth is cooked, the stronger the flavors will be.

Strain the stock and adjust the seasoning. It's advisable to let the stock cool completely so that you can skim off the fat. When cold, the fat will solidify on the surface, so chilled overnight in the refrigerator will make the job very easy. Poultry stock can be used instead of water for many of the recipes in this book. It gives the soups an added flavor which, although not essential, is relished by soup connoisseurs.

### VARIATION
The best beef stock is the liquid from a pot-au-feu. To ensure the stock is full of flavor and has an attractive color, lightly brown the meat and bones before you add the vegetables and water. Beef stock is very fatty, so it's important to skim off all the fat. To do this more easily, chill the stock (after straining) and then remove the solidified fat. The broth from the pot-au-feu is an enjoyable dish by itself, but you can also add extras like potato dumplings.

## vegetable stock

PREPARATION TIME: 15 MINUTES / COOKING TIME: 1 HOUR

**2 carrots**
**1 leek**
**1 zucchini**
**1 onion**
**1 shallot**
**1 stalk celery**
**1 small turnip**
**¼ small cabbage (white or green)**
**1 bouquet garni (1 or 2 spigs thyme and 1 bay leaf, rolled**
 **in a green leek leaf and tied firmly with string)**
**4½ pints (2.5 L) water**
**salt, freshly ground black pepper**

Peel and/or trim and coarsely chop all the vegetables, then put in a high-sided
stockpot. Cover with the measured water, add the bouquet garni, and season sparingly
with salt and pepper. Bring to a boil, skim off any scum with a slotted spoon, then turn
down the heat and simmer for 1 hour. Skim the surface of the liquid regularly. Strain
the stock and skim off any surface residue. Adjust the seasoning to taste, if necessary.

# broths and stocks

## Chinese-style vegetable broth
PREPARATION TIME: 15 MINUTES / COOKING TIME: 1¼ HOURS

2 carrots
1 leek
1 onion
2 shallots
1 stalk celery
1 small turnip
¼ small cabbage (white or green)
1 bouquet garni (1 or 2 thyme sprigs and 1 bay leaf, rolled
   in a green leek leaf and tied firmly with string)
4½ pints (2.5 L) water
Chinese noodles
soy sauce
few sprigs of cilantro
salt, freshly ground black pepper

Peel, trim, and coarsely chop all the vegetables (except 1 of the shallots, which should
be set aside). Put all of the chopped vegetables in a high-sided stockpot. Cover with
the measured water, add the bouquet garni, and season sparingly with salt and
pepper. Bring to a boil, skim off any scum with a slotted spoon, then turn down the
heat and simmer for 1 hour. Skim the liquid regularly. Peel and finely chop the
remaining shallot. Strain the stock and adjust the seasoning, if necessary. Bring the
stock to a boil. Add a few Chinese noodles and the shallot. Lower the heat and simmer
over medium heat until the noodles are well cooked. Before serving, add a few drops
of soy sauce and a little cilantro.

## beef broth with potato dumplings
PREPARATION TIME: 10 MINUTES / COOKING TIME: 30 MINUTES

½ lb (250 g) potatoes, peeled and chopped
½ cup (125 mL) milk
1 egg
⅓ cup (75 mL) all-purpose flour
3 pints (1.5 L) beef stock
salt, freshly ground black pepper

Boil the potatoes in a little salted water until tender.
Strain them well and mash with the milk. Check the
seasoning. Beat in the egg and flour, then shape the
potato dough into a long roll and cut it into sections
1–1½ inches (3–4 cm) long. Poach the dumplings
for about 10 minutes in piping hot beef stock (see
page 114).

## avegolemono (Greek soup)
PREPARATION TIME: 5 MINUTES / COOKING TIME: 10 MINUTES

3 pints (1.5 L) poultry stock
2 eggs
2 Tbsp (30 mL) lemon juice
parsley, leaves stripped and chopped
salt, freshly ground black pepper

Bring the stock to a boil, then turn down the heat to
just maintain a simmer. Whisk the eggs in a bowl with
the lemon juice. Add a little salt and some freshly
ground black pepper. Add a small ladle of stock to the
eggs, while continuing to whisk, then gently pour this
mixture into the rest of the gently simmering stock.
Continue whisking until the egg is cooked. Adjust the
seasoning, to taste, and sprinkle with parsley just
before serving.

## shallot broth
PREPARATION TIME: 10 MINUTES / COOKING TIME: 45 MINUTES

1 tsp (5 mL) olive oil
½ lb (250 g) shallots, peeled and sliced
½ lb (250 g) mild onions (red), peeled and sliced
1 Tbsp (15 mL) granulated sugar
3 pints (1.5 L) poultry stock
1 Tbsp (15 mL) mustard
1 or 2 sprigs tarragon, leaves stripped
salt, freshly ground black pepper

Heat the oil in a deep pan and lightly brown the shallots and onions over very low
heat for 20 minutes. Stir, and add a small amount of water from time to time so that
the vegetables brown slowly without sticking to the base of the pan. Sprinkle with
granulated sugar and continue cooking for another 10 minutes. Add the poultry stock
and bring to a boil. Lower the heat to moderate and simmer for 15 minutes. Before
serving, adjust the seasoning, then add the mustard and the tarragon leaves.

chilled soups and snacks

# chilled soups and snacks

## gazpacho
PREPARATION TIME: 20 MINUTES / CHILLING TIME: 1 HOUR

1 cucumber, washed and trimmed
1 bell pepper (green or yellow), washed, seeded, and cut in small strips
3 lb (1.5 kg) tomatoes, peeled (see page 12), cored, seeded,
    and chopped (or 3 x 16-oz/500-g cans tomatoes)
4 large salad onions, peeled and finely sliced
2 cloves garlic, peeled and finely chopped
1/2 tsp (2 mL) granulated sugar
3 Tbsp (45 mL) olive oil
Tabasco
3 Tbsp (45 mL) balsamic vinegar
3/4 cup (175 mL) water
salt, freshly ground black pepper

Finely dice the cucmber, but leave the peel on. If the skin is very thick, then peel in alternate strips, because it's important to retain a hint of green. Prepare the rest of the vegetables and put them in a large bowl along with the diced cucumber. Add the sugar, oil, Tabasco, and balsamic vinegar. Season with salt and pepper. Blend to a coarse purée, adding the measured water to obtain a liquid consistency, but don't let it become "watery." Check the seasoning, adding more balsamic vinegar or Tabasco, according to taste. Chill in the refrigerator for at least 1 hour before serving.

## why not serve with
## sun-dried tomato cake
PREPARATION TIME: 15 MINUTES / COOKING TIME: 1 HOUR 10 MINUTES

1/2 lb (250 g) all-purpose flour
2 tsp (10 mL) baking powder
4 eggs
3/4 cup plus 2 Tbsp (200 mL) peanut oil
3/4 cup plus 2 Tbsp (200 mL) white wine (or milk)
7 oz (200 g) sun-dried tomatoes, chopped
5 oz (150 g) ham, finely diced
1/2 cup (125 g) grated Parmesan cheese
Salt, freshly ground black pepper

Preheat oven to 375°F (190°C). Sift the flour and baking powder together in a large mixing bowl. Add the eggs and mix thoroughly. Add the oil, followed by the wine, salt, and a little freshly ground black pepper, mixing continuously. When the mixture is smooth, stir in the tomatoes, diced ham, and 2/3 of the cheese. Pour the mixture into an 8 x 4-inch (1.5-L) loaf pan and bake for 1 hour. Sprinkle the remaining Parmesan over the top of the cake and bake for a further 10 minutes. Turn out of the loaf pan immediately and leave to cool on a rack.

## crab gazpacho

PREPARATION TIME: 20 MINUTES / CHILLING TIME: 1 HOUR

1 cucumber, washed and trimmed
1 bell pepper (green or yellow), washed, seeded and cut in thin strips
3 lb (1.5 kg) tomatoes, peeled (see page 12), cored, seeded
  and chopped (or 3 x 16-oz/500-g cans tomatoes)
4 large salad onions, peeled, and sliced
2 cloves garlic, peeled and finely chopped
1/2 tsp (2 mL) granulated sugar
3 Tbsp (45 mL) olive oil
Tabasco
3 Tbsp (45 mL) balsamic vinegar
3/4 cup (175 mL) water
1 x 8 oz (250 g) can crab meat
1 lemon
salt, freshly ground black pepper

Finely dice the cucmber, but leave the peel on. If the skin is very thick, then peel in alternate strips, because it's important to retain a hint of green. Prepare the rest of the vegetables and put them in a large bowl along with the diced cucumber. Add the sugar, oil, Tabasco, and balsamic vinegar. Season with salt and pepper. Blend the soup to a coarse purée, adding the measured water to obtain a liquid consistency, but don't allow it to become "watery." Check the seasoning, adding more vinegar or Tabasco, according to taste. Chill in the refrigerator for at least 1 hour. Just before serving, add the crab meat and mix in thoroughly. Garnish each bowl with a slice of lemon.

## cucumber and dill "smoothie"
PREPARATION TIME: 10 MINUTES / CHILLING TIME: 2 HOURS

**1 cucumber, washed and trimmed**
**2 cups (500 mL) 2% milk**
**1 small sprig dill, coarsely chopped**
**salt, freshly ground black pepper**

Dice the cucumber without removing the skin. Blend to a fine, smooth purée with the milk and dill. Season with salt and pepper. Chill in the refrigerator for 2 hours and serve iced. Mix well before serving to ensure that the "smoothie" is rich and creamy.

VARIATION
Substitute finely chopped fresh mint for the dill.

why not serve with
## marinated salmon (homemade gravlax)
PREPARATION TIME: 25 MINUTES / CHILLING TIME: 48 HOURS

Cucumber and dill go perfectly with all kinds of smoked or marinated fish, like rollmops. It's not hard to marinate the salmon yourself, but you should prepare it at least 48 hours in advance.

**2 tsp (10 mL) freshly ground black pepper**
**1/4 cup (50 mL) granulated sugar**
**1/4 cup (50 mL) sea salt**
**2 lb (1 kg) raw salmon, from the middle part (ask your fish supplier**
  **to cut it in half horizontally and to leave the skin on)**
**1 bunch dill, finely chopped**
**1 lemon**

Mix together the pepper, sugar, and salt. Separate the salmon fillets, lay cut side up and sprinkle them with the marinade mix. Top with a thick layer of dill, then sandwich the fillets together, cut side to cut side. Put on a plate and place inside a plastic bag. Place the plate in the refrigerator and cover the entire surface of the fish with a heavy weight (a cutting board with something heavy placed on top is ideal): this allows the spices to penetrate the flesh of the fish. The following day, turn over the plastic bag, return it to the refrigerator, and replace the "weight." The day after, remove the fillets and cut them into thin slices, leaving the skin on (or, if preferred, not allowing the knife to cut through the skin). Garnish with a little dill and lemon.

# chilled soups and snacks

## vichyssoise

PREPARATION TIME: 15 MINUTES / COOKING TIME: 35 MINUTES / CHILLING TIME: 4 HOURS

1 onion, peeled and finely sliced
1 lb (500 g) leeks (white part only), peeled and finely sliced
2 tsp (10 mL) olive oil
1¼ lb (625 g) potatoes, peeled and chopped
4 cups (1 L) water
1 cup (250 mL) milk
1 cup (250 mL) light cream
chives, chopped
salt, white pepper

Soften the leeks and the onion in a little oil in a deep pan over low heat, taking care not to let them brown as this is a "white" soup. Add the potatoes, measured water, and a little salt. Cover, and simmer over low heat for about 30 minutes. Remove from the heat, and blend thoroughly to obtain a smooth, creamy purée. Gradually add the milk and cream to obtain a good consistency. It's a good idea to keep back some of the milk and cream in the refrigerator and add later.

Chill the soup in the refrigerator for at least 4 hours. Remove from the refrigerator and stir well. This is the time to adjust the soup's consistency by adding the remaining milk and cream if necessary. Adjust the seasoning, to taste. Serve garnished with a sprinkling of chives.

## why not serve with
## blue cheese straws

PREPARATION TIME: 10 MINUTES / COOKING TIME: 10 MINUTES

1 small pack of ready-made flaky pastry
5 oz (150 g) soft blue cheese (if possible, Bleu d'Auvergne,
Bleu des Causses, Fourme d'Ambert)

Preheat oven to 400°F (200°C). Cut the pastry into strips of about ½-¾ inches (1-1.5 cm) wide, then cut these into sections of 1½-2 inches (4-5 cm) long. Remove the rind from the cheese and mash coarsely with a fork. Spread each pastry straw with a little of the mashed cheese. Place them on a lightly floured baking sheet and bake for about 10 minutes: the pastry straws should turn a pale golden color. Allow to cool before serving.

# chilled soups and snacks

## chilled carrot and coconut soup
PREPARATION TIME: 10 MINUTES / COOKING TIME: 35 MINUTES / CHILLING TIME: 4 HOURS

2 lb (1 kg) carrots, peeled and sliced
4 cups (1 L) water
1/2 tsp (2 mL) ground coriander
1/2 tsp (2 mL) ground cumin
1/2 tsp (2 mL) ground cinnamon
2 salad onions, rinsed and chopped
1 cup (250 mL) coconut milk
salt, freshly ground black pepper

Bring the carrots to a boil in the measured water along with all the spices and a little salt. Reduce the heat to low and leave to simmer for about 30 minutes (the carrots should be very soft). Remove from the heat, add the onions and coconut milk, and blend the soup to a very smooth purée. Adjust the seasoning, to taste, leave to cool and then chill in the refrigerator for at least 4 hours.

why not serve with
## wild rice salad with almonds and raisins
PREPARATION TIME: 5 MINUTES / COOKING TIME: 30 MINUTES

1³/4 cups (425 mL) wild rice
4 cups (1 L) water
²/3 cup (150 mL) port
ground coriander
ground cumin
ground cinnamon
1 cup (250 g) raisins
1 cup (250 mL) slivered almonds
salt, freshly ground black pepper

Boil the rice in the measured water with a little salt. In the meantime, heat the port together with 1 pinch each of the spices in a small saucepan. Add the raisins, then turn down the heat and simmer for 5 minutes. Put to one side, but do not drain. Lightly toast the almonds in a dry skillet. Put to one side.

When the rice is cooked, strain, and put the grains into a bowl. Add the raisins along with their cooking liquid, followed by the toasted almonds. Mix well and adjust the seasoning, to taste, if necessary.

## celeriac and apple soup

PREPARATION TIME: 15 MINUTES / COOKING TIME: 40 MINUTES / CHILLING TIME: 4 HOURS

2 tsp (10 mL) olive oil
1 onion, peeled and sliced
3 slightly tart apples (Granny Smith, McIntosh, Boskoop ...),
    peeled, cored, and chopped
1 celeriac (celery root), peeled and chopped
5 cups (1.25 L) water
1 Tbsp (15 mL) lemon juice
nutmeg
1 small bunch chives
salt, freshly ground black pepper

Heat the oil in a deep pan and lightly brown the onions over low heat with the lid on until transparent, then add the chopped applea and celeriac. Mix well and continue cooking for 5 minutes, stirring from time to time. Add the measured water, season with salt and pepper, and simmer for 30 minutes.

When the celeriac is soft, remove from the heat and blend the soup to a very smooth purée. Stir in the lemon juice, a pinch of nutmeg, and adjust the seasoning, to taste. Leave to cool, then chill in the refrigerator for about 4 hours. (If you want to speed up the initial cooling, stand the bowl of soup in a larger bowl of ice water.) Serve the soup garnished with the chives finely snipped with scissors.

# chilled soups and snacks

## summer beet soup
PREPARATION TIME: 10 MINUTES / COOKING TIME: 35 MINUTES / CHILLING TIME: 3 HOURS

**6 medium red beets (uncooked), peeled and diced**
**8 shallots, peeled and sliced**
**4 cups (1 L) water**
**3 oranges**
**2 tsp (10 mL) granulated sugar**
**2 Tbsp (30 mL) balsamic vinegar**
**2/3 cup (150 mL) crème fraîche or sour cream**
**salt, freshly ground black pepper**

Put the beets and shallots in a deep pan and add the measured water. Bring to a boil, then turn down the heat and simmer for about 30 minutes, or until the beets are soft. In the meantime, pare the zest from 1 of the oranges with a zester or sharp knife, cut into very thin slices, and set aside. Squeeze the juice from all 3 oranges.

Remove the pan from the heat and add the orange juice and sugar. Blend the soup to a very smooth purée. Add the balsamic vinegar and season with salt and pepper. Stir in the prepared zest and chill the soup in the refrigerator for at least 3 hours. Serve the soup in bowls topped with a spoonful of crème fraîche or sour cream.

## why not serve with
## cheese puffs
PREPARATION TIME: 15 MINUTES / COOKING TIME: 30 MINUTES

**1 cup (250 mL) water**
**3 oz (80 g) butter**
**1 cup (250 mL) all-purpose flour**
**3 medium-sized eggs**
**5 oz (150 g) grated Gruyère cheese**
**nutmeg**
**salt**

Preheat oven to 350°F (180°C). Put the measured water, butter, and a pinch of salt in a saucepan and bring to a full boil over medium heat. Remove from the heat and add the flour all at once, stirring vigorously with a wooden spoon. Put the pan back on the heat and continue to stir until the dough pulls away from the sides of the pan. Remove from the heat, let cool for a few minutes and then beat in the eggs one at a time, making sure that the choux paste is smooth before adding the next egg. Incorporate 1/2 the grated cheese and a pinch of nutmeg.

Shape the choux paste into small round puffs or a large ring and place on a lightly oiled baking sheet. Sprinkle with the remaining cheese and bake for 20-25 minutes. The cheese puffs can be eaten hot or cold.

# chilled soups and snacks

## chilled cream of curried zucchini soup

PREPARATION TIME: 10 MINUTES / COOKING TIME: 20 MINUTES / CHILLING TIME: 4 HOURS, INCLUDING
2 HOURS PRELIMINARY COOLING

2 lb (1 kg) zucchini, rinsed, trimmed, and sliced
2 salad onions, cleaned and coarsely chopped
2 cups (500 mL) water
1 cup (250 mL) thick, creamy plain yogurt
1 tsp (5 mL) curry powder, strength to taste
1 clove garlic, crushed (optional)
1 Tbsp (15 mL) olive oil
salt, freshly ground black pepper

Put the vegetables in a deep pan with the measured water (which should not
completely cover them as the zucchini already have a high water content). Add a little
salt and simmer over moderate for 15-20 minutes. When the vegetables are soft,
remove from the heat and drain. Blend the soup to a very smooth purée. If necessary,
add a little water: the consistency should be very creamy. Allow to cool for 1-2 hours.
Mix the yogurt, curry powder, garlic (if using), and olive oil together and add to the
zucchini soup. Adjust the seasoning, to taste. Chill for at least another 2 hours.

## why not serve with
## cheese cookies

PREPARATION TIME: 15 MINUTES / COOKING TIME: 10 MINUTES

makes about 20 cookies:
1 cup (250 mL) all-purpose flour
$^1\!/_2$ cup (125 mL) butter
1 cup (250 mL ) grated cheese (Gruyère, Parmesan ...)
salt, freshly ground black pepper

Preheat oven to 400°F (200°C) and lightly grease a baking sheet. In a large mixing
bowl, combine all the ingredients together in a large bowl with your fingertips to
obtain a ball of dough. Roll out the dough to a thickness of about $^1\!/_4$ inch (5 mm),
or thinner. Cut into disks with a cookie cutter or the rim of a tumbler, put the disks
on the baking sheet and bake for about 10 minutes.

Take care! Although the baking time will vary according to the thickness of the dough,
these cookies turn a lovely golden brown very fast.

## chilled cream of spinach and avocado soup
PREPARATION TIME: 10 MINUTES / COOKING TIME: 20 MINUTES / CHILLING TIME: 4 HOURS

**1 tsp (5 mL) olive oil**
**2 onions, peeled and sliced**
**1 lb (500 g) spinach, thoroughly rinsed**
**4 cups (1 L) water**
**2 avocados**
**juice of 1 lime**
**1 cup plain yogurt**
**2 tsp (10 mL) Worcestershire sauce (or soy sauce)**
**salt, freshly ground black pepper**

Heat the olive oil in a large, deep pan and lightly brown the onions for several minutes over gentle heat, then add the spinach for a few minutes to wilt down. Pour in the measured water and add a little salt. Cover, and leave to simmer for about 15 minutes. Remove from the heat and leave to cool.

Peel the avocados, discard the pits, dice the flesh into small cubes, and drizzle with lime juice. Add to the cooled spinach soup, blend to a smooth purée, and add the yogurt. Adjust the seasoning and spice up, to taste, with some Worcestershire sauce. Chill for at least 4 hours before serving.

## why not serve with
## mini bacon and apple sandwiches
PREPARATION TIME: 15 MINUTES

**6 slices of whole-wheat sandwich bread, crusts removed**
**Philadelphia, or any other cream cheese**
**12 spinach leaves, each large enough to cover a slice**
**  of bread, washed and trimmed**
**2 tart eating apples, peeled, cored and each cut**
**  in 12 thin slices**
**12 bacon strips, cut in half across and broiled crisply**

Toast the slices of bread and spread each one with cream cheese. Cover 3 slices with alternate layers starting with 1 spinach leaf, then bacon halves, apple slices, and spinach, repeating until the fillings are finished up, and ending with a spinach leaf. Cover with the remaining slices of toast and cut each sandwich into 4 triangles.

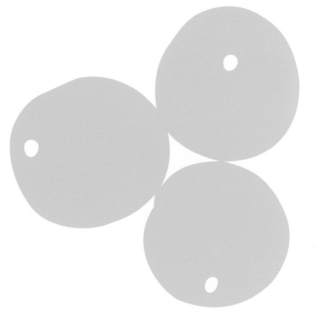

fruit soups

# fruit soups

## chilled cream of melon and cucumber soup
PREPARATION TIME: 15 MINUTES / CHILLING TIME: 1-2 HOURS

1 cucumber, peeled and seeded, except for a small
    piece of one end left unpeeled
2 melons, peeled and seeded
1 Tbsp (15 mL) lemon juice
3 Tbsp (45 mL) balsamic vinegar
salt, freshly ground black pepper

Blend 2/3 of the cucumber together with the melon, lemon juice, and balsamic vinegar
to a very smooth purée. Season with salt and pepper. Chill until just before serving
(at least 1-2 hours). Finely slice the unpeeled cucumber (1 slice per serving) and cut
each slice into quarters. Serve the soup garnished with 4 quarters for each bowl,
placed at the last moment.

TIP
It takes no time at all to make this soup, so it's better not to prepare it too far in
advance. In that case, just keep the melons and cucumber in the refrigerator until
at least 2 hours before the meal.

## blueberry and cinnamon soup
PREPARATION TIME: 10 MINUTES / COOKING TIME: 20 MINUTES /
CHILLING TIME: 4 HOURS

1 1/2 lb (750 g) fresh blueberries,
    thoroughly washed
3 cups (750 mL) water
4 cloves
1 stick cinnamon
1/3 cup (75 mL) honey
1 Tbsp (15 mL) lemon juice
3 Tbsp (45 mL) crème de cassis
    (blackcurrant liqueur)
1 Tbsp (15 mL) red wine vinegar
1 cup (250 mL) plain yogurt

Put aside a small number of the blueberries for
garnish and place the rest into a deep pan. Add the
measured water, cloves, and cinnamon stick and bring
to a boil over low heat. Add the honey, turn down the
heat and simmer partially covered for 15 minutes.
Remove from the heat, take out the cloves and
cinnamon stick, and add the lemon juice, blackcurrant
liqueur, and red wine vinegar. Blend the soup to a very
smooth purée.

Leave aside to cool, then chill in the refrigerator for
at least 4 hours. Serve in chilled bowls and garnish
with a dollop of yogurt and a few blueberries.

## strawberries in wine
PREPARATION TIME: 10 MINUTES / CHILLING TIME:
1-2 HOURS

1 1/2 lb (750 g) ripe, sweet strawberries,
    washed and hulled
1/2 bottle red wine (Loire wine, for example)
balsamic vinegar
1 cup (250 mL) sugar

Halve or quarter the strawberries, depending on their
size, and put them in a mixing bowl. Drizzle with a few
drops of balsamic vinegar, then sprinkle with the
sugar. Pour over the red wine and chill for 1-2 hours.

VARIATION
To spice things up, add 2 or 3 star anise to the wine
and remove before serving, or grind a little high-
quality black pepper over the soup just before serving.

# fruit soups

## nectarine and raspberry soup with basil
PREPARATION TIME: 10 MINUTES / REFRIGERATION TIME: 1 HOUR

**6 very ripe nectarines, washed, pitted, and sliced**
**2 Tbsp (30 mL) lemon juice**
**3/4 lb (350 g) raspberries**
**ice water**
**granulated sugar (if necessary)**
**2 sprigs basil, leaves stripped**

Put the nectarine slices in a bowl and drizzle with the lemon juice. Put 1/3 of the nectarines to one side and purée the rest with a little ice water to obtain a smooth soup. Sprinkle with a little granulated sugar, if necessary. Add the reserved nectarine slices and the raspberries to the soup and chill for at least 1 hour. Garnish with a little shredded basil before serving.

### VARIATION
This soup can be made with very ripe yellow or white peaches, but you'll need to peel them first. This is easy if you dip peaches first in boiling water for 1 minute then refresh them in cold water, but don't peel until you're ready to use them or they'll discolor.

## melon and citrus soup
PREPARATION TIME: 20 MINUTES / CHILLING TIME: 2 HOURS

**2 very sweet melons, peeled and seeded**
**2 oranges**
**1 lime**
**1 half-thumb-sized piece fresh ginger, peeled**
**granulated sugar (if necessary)**
**1 kiwifruit, for garnish**

Put the melon flesh in a mixing bowl. Squeeze the oranges and the lime and add the juice to the melon. Grate the ginger, discard any fibers and add to the melon. Blend the contents of the bowl to a very smooth purée. Taste and add a little granulated sugar if the soup is not sweet enough. Chill for at least 2 hours in the refrigerator. Just before serving, peel and slice the kiwifruit. Cut each slice into 3 or 4 pieces and use as a garnish.

## melon and mango soup
PREPARATION TIME: 15 MINUTES / CHILLING TIME: 1 HOUR

**2 very sweet melons, peeled and seeded**
**2 very ripe mangoes, peeled and chopped**
**1 lemon**
**2 or 3 sprigs mint**
**1/2 cup (125 mL) Muscatel**

Put the melon and mango flesh in a mixing bowl. Squeeze the lemon and add the juice. Add 1/2 the mint leaves. Blend these ingredients into a smooth purée and chill for at least 1 hour in the refrigerator. Just before serving, add the Muscatel and give a quick stir. Garnish with the remaining mint leaves.

## watermelon and feta cheese soup
PREPARATION TIME: 15 MINUTES / CHILLING TIME: 1 HOUR

**1 large slice watermelon, peeled and seeded**
**1 Tbsp (15 mL) lemon juice**
**3 oz (75 g) feta cheese**
**2 basil sprigs, shredded**
**salt, freshly ground black pepper**

Put the watermelon flesh in a bowl and add the lemon juice. Add a little salt, remembering that the feta will add a salty flavor. Blend the soup to a very smooth purée and chill for at least 1 hour. Shortly before serving, chop the feta into small cubes. Sprinkle the watermelon soup with the cheese, then the basil. Add a little freshly ground black pepper and serve immediately.

salad pots

# salad pots

## curried chicken and potato salad
PREPARATION TIME: 15 MINUTES / COOKING TIME: 30 MINUTES

3/4 lb (400 g) small waxy new potatoes,
  peeled and cut in halves or quarters
1 skinless chicken breast, cut into small pieces
1 cup (250 mL) plain yogurt
1 shallot, peeled and chopped
1 tsp (5 mL) mild curry powder
ground coriander
salt

Cook the potatoes in lightly salted water for 20 minutes, or until cooked through when tested with a thin skewer. Drain and leave aside to cool.

Fry the chicken pieces, season with salt and pepper, and put to one side on a piece of paper towel.

Prepare the curry sauce by tipping the yogurt into a bowl and whisking in the shallot, the curry powder, a pinch of coriander, and a pinch of salt. Drizzle the sauce over the potatoes and top with the fried chicken.

# salad pots

## oriental chickpea salad
PREPARATION TIME: 15 MINUTES / COOKING TIME: 10 MINUTES

**1 egg**
**1 x 15-oz can chickpeas, washed and drained**
**12-14 cherry tomatoes, washed and cut in half**
**½ tsp (2 mL) cumin seeds**
**1 Tbsp (15 mL) olive oil**
**1 Tbsp (15 mL) balsamic vinegar**
**1 Tbsp (15 mL) capers**
**1 shallot, peeled and chopped**
**salt, freshly ground black pepper**

Hard-cook the egg for 10 minutes, peel the shell, and chop the egg coarsely. In a bowl, mix together all the ingredients. Season to taste with salt and pepper.

# salad pots

## pasta and arugula salad
PREPARATION TIME: 15 MINUTES / COOKING TIME: 15 MINUTES

½ lb (250 g) large pasta shapes
1 roasted bell pepper (red or yellow), peeled, and finely sliced
3 Tbsp (45 mL) olive oil
balsamic vinegar
ground cumin
1 slice ham, finely chopped
¼ cup (50 mL) pine nuts
small piece Parmesan cheese
2 oz (50 g) arugula leaves, rinsed and dried
salt, freshly ground black pepper

Cook the pasta "al dente" (just to the bite, not overcooked). Drain and leave aside to cool. Lightly fry the bell pepper in a little olive oil for 3 minutes to soften. Prepare a vinaigrette from the olive oil, balsamic vinegar, cumin, salt, and pepper, and stir into the pasta. Add the chopped ham, peppers, and pine nuts. Using a vegetable peeler, make shavings of Parmesan and sprinkle them over the salad. Add the arugula leaves just before serving.

## French lentil and cilantro salad
PREPARATION TIME: 10 MINUTES / COOKING TIME: 40 MINUTES

1¼ cups (200 g) green (French) Puy lentils
olive oil
white wine vinegar
1 apple
handful of white grapes, rinsed
sprigs of cilantro, washed, leaves stripped and coarsely chopped
salt, freshly ground black pepper

Boil the green lentils according to the instructions on the package until thoroughly cooked. Drain and set aside to cool. Prepare a vinaigrette by whisking together the olive oil, wine vinegar, salt, and pepper. Stir the vinaigrette into the lentils. Peel, core, and finely chop the apple, and add to the salad along with the grapes. Sprinkle the chopped cilantro over the salad just before serving.

VARIATION
You can substitute a handful of raisins for the grapes.

## wild rice, prune, and bacon salad
PREPARATION TIME: 20 MINUTES / COOKING TIME: 25 MINUTES

1 cup (250 mL) basmati rice
5 oz (150 g) bacon strips, cut across into batons
3 Tbsp (45 mL) olive oil
1 tsp (5 mL) coarse-grain mustard
1½ Tbsp (22 mL) balsamic vinegar
¼ lb (125 g) large, juicy prunes, pitted, and finely chopped
salt, freshly ground black pepper

Boil the rice in salted water until cooked but not mushy. Drain and leave aside to cool.

In the meantime, lightly fry the bacon pieces in their own fat in a non-stick skillet. Set aside on paper towels. Prepare a vinaigrette by whisking together the olive oil, mustard, balsamic vinegar, salt, and pepper. Stir into the cooled rice, then add the bacon pieces and chopped prunes.

## quinoa tabbouleh
PREPARATION TIME: 10 MINUTES / 15 MINUTES COOKING TIME / CHILLING TIME: 10 MINUTES

1 cup (250 mL) quinoa
1 bunch flat-leaf parsley, rinsed and leaves stripped
2 mint leaves
2 Tbsp (30 mL) olive oil
2 Tbsp (30 mL) lemon juice
10 cherry tomatoes, washed and cut in half
salt, freshly ground black pepper

Cook the quinoa in salted water according to the directions on the package. Drain and set aside in a bowl. Finely chop the parsley and mint leaves. In a small bowl, whisk together the olive oil and lemon juice, and season to taste. Pour over the quinoa and stir in the chopped herbs and cherry tomatoes. Chill for 10 minutes before serving.